I0416727

Copyright 2024 Mike B Lukesaw

1. Chapter 1: Introduction to the Food Truck Industry

- Sub-chapter 1.1: The rise of the food truck phenomenon
- Sub-chapter 1.2: Benefits and challenges of operating a food truck
- Sub-chapter 1.3: Trends and innovations in the food truck business

2. Chapter 2: Market Research and Concept Development

- Sub-chapter 2.1: Identifying your target market
- Sub-chapter 2.2: Analyzing the competition
- Sub-chapter 2.3: Developing a unique food truck concept

3. Chapter 3: Planning and Logistics

- Sub-chapter 3.1: Creating a business plan for your food truck
- Sub-chapter 3.2: Choosing the right truck or trailer
- Sub-chapter 3.3: Navigating permits and regulations

4. Chapter 4: Designing Your Menu

- Sub-chapter 4.1: Crafting a diverse and appealing menu
- Sub-chapter 4.2: Pricing strategies for profitability
- Sub-chapter 4.3: Sourcing quality ingredients and suppliers

5. Chapter 5: Branding and Marketing Strategies

- Sub-chapter 5.1: Building a strong food truck brand
- Sub-chapter 5.2: Leveraging social media for marketing
- Sub-chapter 5.3: Traditional marketing methods for food trucks

6. Chapter 6: Operations and Management

- Sub-chapter 6.1: Staffing and team management
- Sub-chapter 6.2: Inventory management and ordering
- Sub-chapter 6.3: Point-of-sale systems and technology integration

7. Chapter 7: Financial Management

- Sub-chapter 7.1: Budgeting and financial planning

8. Chapter 8: Growing Your Food Truck Business

STARTING A FOOD TRUCK BUSINESS

Chapter 1

Introduction to the Food Truck Industry

1.1: The rise of the food truck phenomenon

The food truck phenomenon represents a dynamic and innovative shift in the culinary landscape, transforming the way people experience and consume food. This movement has gained significant momentum over the past decade, reshaping urban dining scenes and challenging traditional notions of restaurant dining. Several factors have contributed to the rise of the food truck phenomenon.

1. **Entrepreneurial Spirit and Lower Entry Barriers:** The food truck industry is characterized by its entrepreneurial spirit, attracting chefs and cooks eager to showcase their culinary talents without the significant financial investment required for a brick-and-mortar restaurant. The lower entry barriers have allowed a diverse range of individuals to enter the food industry and experiment with unique and niche cuisines.

2. **Flexibility and Mobility:** One of the defining features of food trucks is their mobility. They can set up shop in various locations throughout the day, catering to different audiences and responding to

changing consumer demands. This flexibility enables food truck owners to participate in events, festivals, and markets, reaching a broader customer base compared to traditional restaurants.

3. **Innovative Cuisine and Fusion Trends:** Food trucks are known for their innovative and often experimental approach to cuisine. Many food trucks specialize in fusion cuisine, blending culinary traditions from different cultures to create unique and exciting flavor combinations. This creativity has resonated with consumers seeking novel and Instagram-worthy dining experiences.

4. **Social Media and Digital Marketing:** Social media platforms, such as Instagram, Twitter, and Facebook, have played a pivotal role in the success of food trucks. These platforms provide a cost-effective way for food truck owners to market their offerings, share their locations in real-time, and engage with their customer base. The visually appealing nature of food truck cuisine makes it highly shareable, contributing to the industry's popularity on social media.

5. **Changing Consumer Preferences:** Modern consumers increasingly value convenience, variety, and authenticity. Food trucks align with these preferences by offering quick and accessible meals, diverse menu options, and an intimate, personalized connection between

the customer and the chef. Many consumers appreciate the transparency and authenticity of watching their meals being prepared right in front of them.

6. **Supportive Regulatory Environment:** In many cities, regulations and attitudes toward food trucks have evolved to support the industry's growth. Some municipalities have created designated spaces for food trucks, streamlined permitting processes, and implemented food safety standards to ensure the legitimacy and quality of mobile culinary operations.

7. **Cultural and Economic Impact:** The food truck phenomenon has become more than just a culinary trend; it has become a cultural and economic force. Food trucks contribute to the vibrancy of urban spaces, supporting local economies and creating a sense of community. Additionally, they have become incubators for emerging culinary talent, allowing chefs to experiment, refine their offerings, and potentially transition to permanent restaurant ventures

The rise of the food truck phenomenon reflects a confluence of factors, including entrepreneurship, mobility, culinary innovation, digital marketing, changing consumer preferences, regulatory support, and cultural impact. As this trend continues to evolve, it is likely that food trucks will remain a dynamic and integral part of the modern culinary landscape.

Benefits of Operating a Food Truck:

1. **Lower Initial Investment:** One of the primary advantages of starting a food truck business is the significantly lower initial investment compared to a traditional brick-and-mortar restaurant. Entrepreneurs can enter the food industry with a smaller budget, making it a more accessible option for those with limited capital.

2. **Mobility and Flexibility:** Food trucks are mobile, allowing owners to reach different locations and cater to diverse audiences. This mobility provides flexibility to participate in events, festivals, and high-traffic areas, optimizing sales and exposure.

3. **Direct Customer Interaction:** Food trucks offer a unique opportunity for direct interaction between chefs or owners and customers. This personal connection can help build a loyal customer base, receive immediate feedback, and adjust the menu based on customer preferences.

4. **Innovative Culinary Expression:** Operating a food truck allows chefs to experiment with creative and innovative

culinary concepts. The limited space encourages efficiency and specialization, fostering unique and often trend-setting menu items.

5. **Social Media Marketing:** The visually appealing nature of food truck cuisine makes it highly shareable on social media platforms. Owners can leverage these platforms for cost-effective marketing, engaging with their audience, and announcing their locations in real-time.

6. **Adaptability to Trends:** Food trucks can quickly adapt to emerging food trends and consumer preferences. This agility enables owners to stay competitive and relevant, adjusting their menu and offerings based on changing culinary and dietary trends.

7. **Lower Overhead Costs:** Compared to traditional restaurants, food trucks generally have lower overhead costs. Expenses related to utilities, rent, and maintenance are typically reduced, contributing to a potentially higher profit margin.

Challenges of Operating a Food Truck:

1. **Limited Space and Storage:** The compact size of food trucks can be a significant challenge. Limited kitchen and storage space

may restrict the variety of menu items and require careful inventory management.

2. **Weather Dependence:** Food truck operations are heavily influenced by weather conditions. Adverse weather, such as rain or extreme heat, can impact sales and make it challenging to operate, especially in outdoor locations.

3. **Permitting and Regulations:** Navigating the complex web of permits, licenses, and health regulations can be a time-consuming and bureaucratic process. Compliance with local regulations is essential and may vary from one location to another.

4. **Equipment Reliability:** The reliance on mobile cooking equipment means that breakdowns or malfunctions can disrupt operations. Regular maintenance and having backup plans in place are crucial to minimize downtime.

5. **Competition and Saturation:** As the food truck industry continues to grow, competition in certain markets can become intense. Finding unique selling points and differentiating from competitors can be challenging, particularly in areas with a high concentration of food trucks.

6. **Limited Operating Hours:** Food trucks often have limited operating hours, especially if they focus on lunch or late-night crowds. This constraint may restrict revenue potential

compared to restaurants that can operate throughout the day.

7. **Parking Challenges:** Finding suitable and legal parking spaces can be a persistent challenge. Some locations may have strict regulations, and competition for prime parking spots in popular areas can be fierce.

8. **Seasonal Fluctuations:** Seasonal changes can significantly impact business. For example, outdoor locations may see reduced foot traffic during colder months, leading to fluctuations in revenue.

While operating a food truck offers various benefits, entrepreneurs must navigate these challenges to build a successful and sustainable business. Adaptability, effective marketing, and a keen understanding of local regulations are crucial for overcoming the hurdles of the food truck industry.

Trends and innovations in the food truck business
  • **Culinary Fusion:**
    • Many food trucks are experimenting with fusion cuisine, combining different culinary traditions to create unique and exciting flavor profiles. This allows for a diverse menu that appeals to a broad range of tastes.

- **Healthy and Sustainable Options:**
  - With the increasing focus on health and sustainability, food trucks are incorporating more plant-based and locally sourced ingredients into their menus. This trend aligns with the growing demand for healthier food choices.
- **Technology Integration:**
  - Food trucks are leveraging technology to streamline operations and enhance the customer experience. Mobile apps for ordering, cashless payment options, and social media marketing are becoming standard practices.
- **Specialized Diets:**
  - Food trucks are catering to specialized diets such as gluten-free, keto, vegan, and others. This allows them to tap into niche markets and cater to a broader customer base.
- **Gourmet Offerings:**
  - The perception of food trucks as providers of quick and cheap eats is changing. Many food truck owners are focusing on gourmet offerings, presenting high-quality dishes that rival those found in traditional restaurants.
- **Branding and Unique Themes:**

- Successful food trucks often have a strong brand identity and a unique theme. This could include eye-catching graphics, memorable names, and a consistent visual presence on social media platforms.
- **Data Analytics:**
  - Some food trucks are utilizing data analytics to understand customer preferences, track sales, and optimize their menus. This information helps them make data-driven decisions to improve efficiency and profitability.
- **Alcohol Pairings:**
  - To enhance the overall dining experience, some food trucks are collaborating with local breweries or wineries to offer alcohol pairings with their dishes. This creates a more sophisticated and enjoyable experience for customers.
- **Community Engagement:**
  - Successful food trucks often engage with their local communities through events, partnerships, and social media. Building a loyal customer base is crucial for sustained success in the competitive food truck industry.
- **Pop-Up Collaborations:**
  - Food trucks are increasingly collaborating with other businesses or

chefs for pop-up events. This allows them to offer unique menu items and reach new audiences.

- **Dessert and Specialty Items:**
  - Some food trucks specialize in desserts or unique items, catering to customers with a sweet tooth or those looking for something different from the usual savory options.
- **Innovative Marketing Strategies:**
  - Beyond social media, food trucks are exploring innovative marketing strategies such as influencer collaborations, interactive promotions, and even participation in food festivals to increase visibility and attract customers.

As the food truck industry continues to grow and adapt to changing consumer preferences, new trends and innovations will likely emerge. Entrepreneurs in this space should stay adaptable and open to embracing new ideas to stay ahead in this dynamic market.

Chapter 2

Market Research and Concept Development

2.1: Identifying your target market

An important first step in any business planning process is determining your target market. Knowing who your consumers are will help you customize your offerings in terms of goods, services, and marketing to suit their requirements and tastes. Here's a comprehensive how-to guide for determining your target market:

1. Market Research:

- **Demographics:** Start by gathering demographic information about potential customers. This includes age, gender, income level, education, occupation, and location. This data helps create a basic profile of your target audience.
- **Psychographics:** Dig deeper into the lifestyle, values, interests, and behaviors of your potential customers. This information provides insights into their motivations and purchasing decisions.
- **Market Size:** Determine the overall size of your target market. Understanding the potential number of customers allows you to

assess the business opportunity and market demand.

2. Customer Surveys and Feedback:

- Conduct surveys and collect feedback from your existing customers or a sample of your target audience. Ask about their preferences, pain points, and what influences their buying decisions. This firsthand information is invaluable for refining your target market.

3. Competitor Analysis:

- Analyze your competitors and identify who they are targeting. Look for gaps or underserved segments that you can tap into. Differentiating your product or service can be easier if you find a niche market that is not adequately addressed.

4. Social Media Insights:

- Utilize social media analytics to understand the demographics and behaviors of your followers or potential audience. Platforms like Facebook, Instagram, and Twitter provide insights into the age, location, and interests of your audience.

5. Google Analytics and Website Data:

- If you have a website, analyze the data using tools like Google Analytics. Understand where your website traffic is coming from, which pages are popular, and demographic information about your online visitors.

6. Industry Reports and Studies:

- Explore industry reports and studies related to your business. These documents often provide valuable data on market trends, consumer behaviors, and the overall landscape. Government publications, trade associations, and market research firms can be good sources.

7. Focus Groups:

- Organize focus groups to gather qualitative data. This involves bringing together a small group of individuals to discuss their thoughts, feelings, and perceptions about your product or service. This can provide rich insights into customer attitudes.

8. Networking and Outreach:

- To meet possible clients, go to trade exhibits, industry gatherings, and networking events. Talk to people, make inquiries, and take note of those who express interest in what you have to offer.

9. Review Your Existing Customer Base:

- Examine your present clientele. Determine the traits that your most profitable and devoted clients have in common. This data can assist you in identifying comparable people or companies.

10. Adaptability and Refinement:

- Understand that your target market may evolve over time. Stay adaptable and be open to refining your target audience based on changing market conditions, industry trends, or shifts in consumer behavior.

11. Create Customer Personas:

- Using the data acquired, create comprehensive customer personas. These fictional characters represent your ideal customers and help in visualizing and understanding their needs, preferences, and behaviors.

12. Test and Iterate:

- Implement your strategies with a targeted approach and evaluate the results. If needed, be prepared to iterate and refine your target market based on real-world feedback and data.

By investing time and effort into identifying your target market, you lay a solid foundation for the success of your business. This process not only helps you tailor your products and services but also allows you to create more effective marketing strategies that resonate with your audience.

2.2: Analyzing the competition

Analyzing the competition is a crucial aspect of strategic planning for any business. It involves evaluating the strengths and weaknesses of competitors to identify opportunities and threats in the market. This process provides valuable insights that can help a company make informed decisions, refine its strategy, and gain a competitive advantage. Here's a detailed breakdown of how to effectively analyze the competition:

1. Identify Competitors:

- **Direct Competitors:** Businesses that cater to the same target market with comparable goods or services.
- **Indirect Competitors:** Those providing alternatives that fulfill the same need or serve a similar purpose.
- **Future Competitors:** Emerging companies or potential entrants into the market.

2. Gather Information:

- **Company Background:** Understand the history, mission, values, and overall objectives of each competitor.
- **Products/Services:** Analyze the range, quality, features, and pricing of their offerings.
- **Market Share:** Determine the market share of each competitor and how it has changed over time.
- **Financials:** Review financial statements, revenue trends, and profitability.
- **Customer Base:** Identify the target audience and the strategies used to attract and retain customers.
- **Distribution Channels:** Evaluate how products or services are delivered to customers.
- **Marketing and Branding:** Examine their marketing strategies, messaging, and brand positioning.
- **SWOT Analysis:** Conduct a SWOT analysis for each competitor (Strengths, Weaknesses, Opportunities, Threats).

3. Benchmarking:

- **Compare Performance:** Benchmark your own performance against competitors in key

areas such as sales, market share, and customer satisfaction.
- **Best Practices:** Identify industry best practices and evaluate how well your competitors adhere to them.

4. Competitive Positioning:

- **Unique Selling Proposition (USP):** Determine the unique aspects that set your competitors apart.
- **Price Positioning:** Understand their pricing strategy and how it compares to yours.
- **Product Differentiation:** Analyze features, quality, and innovation to identify points of differentiation.
- **Brand Perception:** Assess how customers perceive competitor brands compared to yours.

5. Market Trends:

- **Industry Analysis:** Understand broader industry trends, technological advancements, and regulatory changes.
- **Customer Preferences:** Identify shifts in customer preferences and behavior.
- **Innovation:** Evaluate competitors' commitment to innovation and their success in adopting new technologies.

6. Risk Assessment:

- **External Risks:** Identify external factors that could impact competitors (economic conditions, regulatory changes, etc.).
- **Internal Risks:** Assess internal vulnerabilities, such as management issues or financial instability.

7. Customer Feedback:

- **Reviews and Testimonials:** Analyze customer reviews and testimonials for insights into competitors' strengths and weaknesses.
- **Customer Surveys:** Conduct surveys or analyze existing ones to understand customer satisfaction with competitors.

8. Adaptation and Strategy Formulation:

- **Strategic Response:** Develop strategies to counter or capitalize on the identified strengths and weaknesses of competitors.
- **Continuous Monitoring:** Regularly update your analysis to adapt to changes in the competitive landscape.

9. Collaboration Opportunities:

- **Partnerships or Alliances:** Identify potential collaboration opportunities that can benefit both your company and competitors.

10. Ethical Considerations:

- **Compliance and Ethics:** Ensure your analysis and response adhere to ethical standards and legal considerations.

By systematically analyzing the competition, businesses can make informed decisions, enhance their competitive advantage, and position themselves for long-term success in the marketplace. Regularly updating this analysis is crucial, given the dynamic nature of markets and industries.

2.3: Developing a unique food truck concept

Developing a unique food truck concept involves a combination of creativity, market research, and a deep understanding of your target audience. Here's a detailed guide on how to go about creating a distinctive and successful food truck concept:

1. Market Research:

- **Identify Trends:** Stay informed about current food and culinary trends. Understand what is popular among your target demographic.

- **Local Preferences:** Take into account the culinary scene and customs in your area. Find any holes or unfulfilled demands in the market.
- **Competitor Analysis**: Look at current eateries and food trucks to identify a distinct niche and prevent duplication.

2. Define Your Niche:

- **Specialization:** Decide on a specific cuisine, theme, or culinary focus that sets you apart.
- **Unique Selling Proposition (USP):** Determine what will make your food truck stand out. It could be a signature dish, a unique cooking technique, or a theme that resonates with your target audience.

3. Create a Memorable Brand:

- **Brand Identity:** Develop a strong and memorable brand identity, including a catchy name, logo, and color scheme.
- **Storytelling:** Craft a compelling story or theme that aligns with your concept. This can create an emotional connection with customers.

4. Menu Innovation:

- **Signature Dishes:** Create a few standout dishes that reflect your concept and leave a lasting impression.
- **Flexibility:** Keep the menu simple but versatile. Consider dietary restrictions and offer customization options.
- **Seasonal Offerings:** Introduce seasonal or limited-time offerings to keep the menu fresh and exciting.

5. Quality Ingredients and Preparation:

- **Source Locally:** Whenever possible, use locally sourced and fresh ingredients. This not only supports local businesses but also adds authenticity to your concept.
- **Emphasize Quality:** Focus on delivering high-quality food consistently. Attention to detail in preparation and presentation can elevate your food truck's reputation.

6. Innovative Marketing:

- **Social Media Presence:** Use social media sites to spread the word. Post behind-the-scenes photos, provide menu changes, and interact with your audience.
- **Food Photography:** For use in advertisements and social media posts, spend money on excellent food photography

- **Events and Collaborations:** To boost exposure, take part in neighborhood gatherings, work with other companies, and provide a hand with charitable endeavors.

7. **Operational Efficiency:**

- **Streamlined Operations:** Design an efficient and well-organized kitchen layout to optimize workflow.
- **Technology Integration:** Consider using technology for order-taking, payments, and customer engagement to enhance the overall customer experience.

8. Customer Feedback and Adaptation:

- **Collect Feedback:** Actively seek feedback from customers to understand their preferences and make necessary adjustments.
- **Adapt to Trends:** Stay flexible and be willing to adapt your concept based on changing trends and customer feedback.

9. Compliance and Licensing:

- **Health and Safety Standards:** Ensure that your food truck meets all health and safety standards. Obtain the necessary licenses and permits.
- **Local Regulations:** Familiarize yourself with local regulations governing food trucks, parking, and operation.

10. Community Engagement:

- **Build Relationships:** Engage with the local community. Build relationships with customers, other food vendors, and businesses in the area.
- **Sustainability:** Consider incorporating sustainable practices in your operations, which can resonate well with environmentally conscious consumers.

Developing a unique food truck concept requires a balance between creativity and practicality. By conducting thorough market research, creating a memorable brand, offering innovative menu options, and staying engaged with the community, you can establish a distinctive and successful presence in the competitive food truck industry.

Chapter 3

Planning and Logistics

3.1: Creating a business plan for your food truck

Creating a comprehensive business plan is a crucial step in establishing and running a successful food truck business. A well-thought-out plan not only serves as a roadmap for your venture but also helps secure funding and provides a strategic framework for operational decisions. Here's a detailed guide on creating a business plan for your food truck:

1. Executive Summary:

- **Business Name and Concept:** Clearly state the name of your food truck and provide a brief overview of your concept.
- **Mission Statement:** Define the purpose and values of your business.
- **Founding Date and Location:** Specify when and where your food truck will operate.

2. Business Description:

- **Concept and Cuisine:** Detail your food truck concept, the type of cuisine you'll offer, and what makes your truck unique.
- **Target Market:** Identify your target demographic, including age, location, and preferences.
- **Competitive Advantage:** Highlight what sets your food truck apart from competitors.

3. Market Analysis:

- **Industry Overview:** Provide an overview of the food truck industry, including current trends, market size, and growth potential.
- **Target Market Analysis:** Conduct a thorough analysis of your target market, including demographics, buying behavior, and preferences.
- **Competitor Analysis:** Identify and analyze direct and indirect competitors, noting their strengths and weaknesses.

4. Organizational Structure:

- **Ownership Structure:** Specify whether your food truck is a sole proprietorship, partnership, LLC, or corporation.
- **Management Team:** Introduce key team members, their roles, and relevant experience.

- **Advisory Board:** If applicable, mention any advisors or mentors contributing to your business.

5. Products and Services:

- **Menu Overview:** Provide a detailed description of your menu items, pricing strategy, and any unique offerings.
- **Ingredients and Sourcing:** Discuss where you'll source ingredients and emphasize any commitment to quality or local products.

6. Marketing and Sales Strategy:

- **Target Customer Profile:** Clearly define your ideal customer and tailor your marketing efforts accordingly.
- **Promotional Activities:** Outline your marketing plan, including online presence, social media strategy, and promotional events.
- **Pricing Strategy:** Detail how you'll set prices, considering costs, market demand, and perceived value.

7. Operational Plan:

- **Location and Facilities:** Specify where your food truck will operate, including potential locations and any agreements with property owners.

- **Equipment and Technology:** List the equipment you'll need and describe any technology, like point-of-sale systems or food delivery apps.
- **Supply Chain Management:** Detail your supply chain, from ingredient sourcing to inventory management.

8. Regulatory Compliance:

- **Permits and Licenses:** Identify all necessary permits and licenses required to operate your food truck legally.
- **Health and Safety Standards:** Outline your commitment to meeting and exceeding health and safety regulations.

9. Financial Plan:

- **Startup Costs:** Estimate the initial investment required for your food truck, including purchasing or leasing the vehicle, equipment, permits, and initial inventory.
- **Revenue Projections:** Provide detailed revenue projections based on your pricing strategy, market demand, and sales forecasts.
- **Operating Expenses:** Break down monthly operating expenses, including food costs,

staff wages, fuel, maintenance, and marketing expenses.

- **Profit and Loss Statement:** Present a detailed profit and loss statement for the first few years of operation.

10. Risk Analysis and Contingency Plan:

- **Identify Risks:** Assess potential risks to your food truck business, such as changes in regulations, market trends, or unexpected events.
- **Contingency Plans:** Outline strategies to mitigate risks and respond to unexpected challenges.

11. Appendix:

- **Additional Documentation:** Include any supporting documents, such as resumes of key team members, sample menus, lease agreements, or letters of support from potential suppliers.

12. Timeline:

- **Launch Plan:** Develop a timeline for launching your food truck, including key milestones and tasks.

13. Exit Strategy:

- **Long-Term Vision:** Discuss your long-term vision for the food truck business and potential exit strategies if you decide to sell or expand.

Remember, a business plan is a living document that should be revisited and updated regularly as your food truck business evolves. It serves as a guide for decision-making and can be a valuable tool when seeking funding or partnerships.

3.2: Choosing the right truck or trailer

Choosing the right truck or trailer is a critical decision in the food truck business. The vehicle you select will impact your operational efficiency, capacity, and overall success. Here's a detailed guide on how to choose the right truck or trailer for your food truck business:

1. Type of Vehicle:

- **Food Truck vs. Food Trailer:** Choose between a food trailer that can be towed or a self-contained food truck. Every choice has benefits and drawbacks.
  - **Food Truck:** All-in-one unit with an integrated kitchen and driving capability.
  - **Food Trailer:** Towed behind a vehicle, providing flexibility in choosing the

towing vehicle and detachment for stationary service.

2. Size and Layout:

- **Kitchen Space:** Assess the size of the kitchen space and how well it accommodates your menu and cooking equipment.
- **Storage:** Ensure there's enough storage space for ingredients, utensils, and other necessary items.
- **Workflow:** Design the layout to facilitate a smooth workflow, minimizing congestion and optimizing efficiency.

3. Equipment Compatibility:

- **Appliance Fit:** Confirm that your cooking equipment and appliances fit seamlessly into the truck or trailer's layout.
- **Power Supply:** Check if the vehicle can support the power requirements of your kitchen equipment.

4. Condition of the Vehicle:

- **New vs. Used:** Consider whether to buy a new or used vehicle. A new one may come with warranties but can be more expensive, while a used vehicle may require more maintenance.

- **Mechanical Inspection:** Have a qualified mechanic inspect the vehicle for any mechanical issues or needed repairs.

5. Compliance and Regulations:

- **Health and Safety Standards:** Ensure the vehicle complies with health and safety regulations for food service establishments.
- **Local Codes:** Check local regulations regarding food trucks and trailers to ensure compliance.

6. Mobility and Accessibility:

- **Maneuverability:** Consider the vehicle's size and maneuverability, especially if you plan to operate in urban areas with tight spaces.
- **Accessibility:** Ensure the vehicle is accessible to customers, with a clear serving window or counter.

7. Customization Options:

- **Custom vs. Pre-built:** Decide if you want a custom-built vehicle tailored to your specifications or a pre-built model.
- **Branding:** Consider whether the vehicle design allows for effective branding and visibility.

8. Budget Considerations:

- **Cost of Purchase:** Determine your budget for acquiring the vehicle. This includes the purchase price as well as any modifications or customization.
- **Financing Options:** Explore financing options or leasing agreements if purchasing outright is not feasible.

9. Maintenance and Upkeep:

- **Maintenance History:** If buying a used vehicle, review its maintenance history to assess its overall condition.
- **Ease of Maintenance:** Consider the ease of maintenance and availability of replacement parts for the chosen vehicle.

10. Future Expansion:

- **Scalability:** Assess whether the chosen vehicle allows for future expansion, such as adding new equipment or accommodating menu changes.
- **Upgradability:** Consider if the vehicle can be easily upgraded or modified to meet evolving business needs.

11. Insurance Considerations:

- **Insurance Costs:** Investigate insurance costs for the chosen vehicle, including coverage for the vehicle itself and liability insurance.

12. Test Drive and User Feedback:

- **Test Drive:** If possible, take the vehicle for a test drive to assess its performance and handling.
- **User Feedback:** Seek feedback from other food truck operators who have used similar vehicles.

13. Resale Value:

- **Depreciation:** Consider the potential resale value of the vehicle, especially if you plan to upgrade or expand your fleet in the future.

14. Warranty and Support:

- **Manufacturer's Warranty:** Check if the vehicle comes with a manufacturer's warranty, and understand its terms and coverage.
- **Support Services:** Investigate the availability of support services from the manufacturer or dealer.

Choosing the right truck or trailer for your food truck business involves careful consideration of your specific needs, regulatory requirements, and future plans. Take the time to thoroughly research and assess each option to make an informed decision that aligns with your business goals and operational requirements.

3.3: Navigating permits and regulations

Navigating permits and regulations is a crucial aspect of launching and operating a food truck business. Compliance with local, state, and federal regulations is essential for ensuring the safety of your customers and staff, as well as avoiding legal issues that could harm your business. Here's a detailed guide on how to navigate permits and regulations for your food truck:

1. Understand Local Regulations:

- **City and County Regulations:** Research and understand the specific regulations governing food trucks in your city and county. Regulations may include zoning laws, parking restrictions, and operational guidelines.
- **Permitting Authorities:** Identify the local health department, fire department, and other relevant authorities responsible for issuing permits.

2. Health Department Permits:

- **Food Handler's Permit:** Ensure that all staff members handling food obtain the necessary food handler's permits or certifications.
- **Mobile Food Vendor Permit:** Obtain a mobile food vendor permit from the local health department, which typically involves inspections of the food truck's kitchen facilities.

3. Vehicle and Operational Permits:

- **Vehicle Inspection:** Schedule a vehicle inspection to ensure it complies with safety and emissions standards.
- **Business License:** Obtain a business license from the local city or county government.
- **Fire Department Approval:** In some jurisdictions, you may need approval from the fire department to operate a mobile food business.

4. Compliance with Food Safety Standards:

- **Food Safety Training:** Ensure that you and your staff undergo food safety training to handle, store, and prepare food safely.
- **HACCP Plan:** Develop a Hazard Analysis and Critical Control Points (HACCP) plan to

identify and control potential food safety hazards.

5. Parking and Zoning Regulations:

- **Parking Permits:** Check if you need specific permits for parking in certain locations or events.
- **Zoning Compliance:** Ensure that your food truck complies with local zoning regulations. Some areas may have restrictions on where food trucks can operate.

6. Insurance Requirements:

- **Liability Insurance:** Obtain liability insurance to protect your business in case of accidents or injuries.
- **Vehicle Insurance:** Ensure your food truck has comprehensive vehicle insurance coverage.

7. Tax Obligations:

- **Sales Tax:** Understand your responsibilities regarding sales tax collection and remittance.
- **Business Income Tax:** Consult with a tax professional to determine your business income tax obligations.

8. Federal Regulations:

- **Employer Identification Number (EIN):** Obtain an EIN from the IRS for tax reporting purposes.
- **FDA Registration:** If applicable, register with the U.S. Food and Drug Administration (FDA), especially if your menu includes certain food products.

9. Community Engagement and Approvals:

- **Community Approval:** Engage with the local community and seek their support, especially if you plan to operate in residential areas.
- **Event Permits:** Obtain permits for participating in events or festivals, which may have their own set of regulations.

10. Renewal and Compliance Monitoring:

- **Renewal Timelines:** Be aware of the expiration dates for your permits and licenses and initiate the renewal process in a timely manner.
- **Regular Inspections:** Proactively schedule and participate in regular inspections to ensure ongoing compliance with health and safety standards.

11. Stay Informed About Changes:

- **Regulatory Updates:** Regularly check for updates and changes in regulations at the local, state, and federal levels.
- **Industry Associations:** Join food truck associations or networks that may provide valuable information and support.

12. Legal Consultation:

- **Legal Advice:** If needed, consult with a legal professional familiar with food service regulations to ensure full compliance.

Navigating permits and regulations requires diligence, attention to detail, and proactive engagement with regulatory bodies. Establishing a good working relationship with local authorities can be beneficial for your food truck business, as they can provide guidance and support throughout the permitting process. Additionally, staying informed about changes and seeking professional advice when needed will contribute to the long-term success of your food truck venture.

Chapter 4

Designing Your Menu

4.1: Crafting a diverse and appealing menu

Navigating permits and regulations is a crucial aspect of launching and operating a food truck business. Compliance with local, state, and federal regulations is essential for ensuring the safety of your customers and staff, as well as avoiding legal issues that could harm your business. Here's a detailed guide on how to navigate permits and regulations for your food truck:

1. Understand Local Regulations:

- **City and County Regulations:** Research and understand the specific regulations governing food trucks in your city and county. Regulations may include zoning laws, parking restrictions, and operational guidelines.
- **Permitting Authorities:** Identify the local health department, fire department, and other relevant authorities responsible for issuing permits.

2. Health Department Permits:

- **Food Handler's Permit:** Ensure that all staff members handling food obtain the necessary food handler's permits or certifications.
- **Mobile Food Vendor Permit:** Obtain a mobile food vendor permit from the local health department, which typically involves inspections of the food truck's kitchen facilities.

3. Vehicle and Operational Permits:

- **Vehicle Inspection:** Schedule a vehicle inspection to ensure it complies with safety and emissions standards.
- **Business License:** Obtain a business license from the local city or county government.
- **Fire Department Approval:** In some jurisdictions, you may need approval from the fire department to operate a mobile food business.

4. Compliance with Food Safety Standards:

- **Food Safety Training:** Ensure that you and your staff undergo food safety training to handle, store, and prepare food safely.
- **HACCP Plan:** To recognise and manage possible risks to food safety, create a Hazard Analysis and Critical Control Points (HACCP) plan.

5. Zoning and Parking Rules:

- • Parking Permits: Find out if you require a special permit to park at particular venues or during particular events.

-

- • Zoning Compliance: Verify that the zoning laws in your area are followed by your food truck. There can be limitations on where food trucks can operate in some places.

6. Insurance Requirements:

- **Liability Insurance:** Obtain liability insurance to protect your business in case of accidents or injuries.
- **Vehicle Insurance:** Ensure your food truck has comprehensive vehicle insurance coverage.

7. Tax Obligations:

- **Sales Tax:** Understand your responsibilities regarding sales tax collection and remittance.
- **Business Income Tax:** Consult with a tax professional to determine your business income tax obligations.

8. Federal Regulations:

- **Employer Identification Number (EIN):** • Employer Identification Number (EIN): To use for tax reporting, get an EIN from the IRS.

- **FDA Registration:** If applicable, register with the U.S. Food and Drug Administration (FDA), especially if your menu includes certain food products.

9. Community Engagement and Approvals:

- **Community Approval:** Engage with the local community and seek their support, especially if you plan to operate in residential areas.
- **Event Permits:** Obtain permits for participating in events or festivals, which may have their own set of regulations.

10. Renewal and Compliance Monitoring:

- **Renewal Timelines:** Be aware of the expiration dates for your permits and licenses and initiate the renewal process in a timely manner.
- **Regular Inspections:** Proactively schedule and participate in regular inspections to ensure ongoing compliance with health and safety standards.

11. Stay Informed About Changes:

- **Regulatory Updates:** Regularly check for updates and changes in regulations at the local, state, and federal levels.
- **Industry Associations:** Join food truck associations or networks that may provide valuable information and support.

12. Legal Consultation:

- **Legal Advice:** If needed, consult with a legal professional familiar with food service regulations to ensure full compliance.

Pricing strategies for profitability

Pricing strategies are crucial for the profitability of any business, and food truck operations are no exception. Developing a well-thought-out pricing strategy requires consideration of various factors, including costs, competition, perceived value, and customer behavior. Here's a detailed guide on pricing strategies for profitability in the context of a food truck business:

1. Cost-Based Pricing:

- **Cost Analysis:** Calculate all direct and indirect costs associated with operating your food truck, including food ingredients, labor, fuel, maintenance, permits, and insurance.

- **Markup:** Add a desired profit margin on top of your costs to determine the selling price. Common markup percentages range from 30% to 50%.

2. Competitive Pricing:

- **Market Research:** Research the pricing strategies of your competitors to understand the market benchmark. Consider how your prices compare to similar offerings in your area.
- **Price Positioning:** Decide whether you want to position your food truck as a premium, mid-range, or budget option based on your target market and the perceived value of your offerings.

3. Value-Based Pricing:

- **Perceived Value:** Set prices based on the perceived value of your food and service. This approach involves understanding what customers are willing to pay for the unique value your food truck provides.
- **Differentiation:** Emphasize what makes your food truck special, such as high-quality ingredients, unique recipes, or exceptional customer service.

4. Dynamic Pricing:

- **Seasonal Pricing:** Modify costs in accordance with demand patterns. For instance, you may provide exclusive discounts during off-peak periods or premium rates during busy periods.
- • Event Pricing: Considering increased foot traffic and demand, consider modifying costs for big events or festivals.

5. Pricing for Bundles:

- **Combo Deals**: To entice buyers to buy more than one item, provide packaged offerings or combination deals. The average transaction value may rise as a result of this.
- **Meal Deals**: Provide meal combinations at a reduced price to entice people to purchase a full meal as opposed to individual products.

6. Psychological Pricing:

- **Pricing Endings:** Use pricing endings like $9.99 instead of $10. This is a psychological tactic that can make prices appear lower to customers.
- **Tiered Pricing:** Offer different pricing tiers (e.g., small, medium, large) to influence customer perception of value.

7. Time-Based Pricing:

- **Happy Hour or Daily Specials:** Introduce discounted prices during specific times to attract customers during slower periods.
- **Early-Bird Specials:** Offer special deals for customers who visit during the early hours.

8. Cost-Plus Pricing:

- **Variable Costs:** Identify variable costs associated with each item on your menu and add a percentage for overhead and profit.
- **Consistency:** This method ensures that you cover all costs while providing consistent pricing for each item.

9. Loss Leader Pricing:

- **Strategic Losses:** Offer a few items at a lower price (loss leaders) to attract customers. Make profits on complementary items or higher-margin offerings.
- **Customer Loyalty:** This strategy can build customer loyalty and encourage repeat business.

10. Subscription or Loyalty Programs:

- **Discounts for Regular Customers:** Implement loyalty programs that reward

repeat customers with discounts or free items after a certain number of purchases.
- **Subscription Services:** Offer subscription-based services where customers pay a fixed fee for a set number of meals per month.

11. Consider External Factors:

- **Economic Conditions:** Be aware of economic factors that may affect your customers' purchasing power. Adjust pricing strategies accordingly during economic fluctuations.
- **Inflation:** Regularly review and adjust prices to account for inflation and rising costs.

12. Testing and Adjusting:

- **Trial Periods:** Periodically test new pricing strategies for specific items or during certain periods to gauge customer response.
- **Feedback Analysis:** Gather customer feedback on pricing and adjust strategies based on their preferences and expectations.

13. Transparency:

- **Transparent Pricing:** Be transparent about your pricing. Clearly communicate the value customers receive in exchange for their money.

- **Avoid Hidden Fees:** Minimize or eliminate hidden fees that could lead to customer dissatisfaction.

14. Regular Review and Adaptation:

- **Market Changes:** Regularly review your pricing strategies in response to changes in the market, customer preferences, and operating costs.
- **Competitor Moves:** Stay informed about changes in competitors' pricing and adjust your strategies accordingly.

Developing a profitable pricing strategy for your food truck requires a balance between covering costs, providing value to customers, and remaining competitive in the market. Regularly monitor and adjust your pricing strategies based on market conditions and customer feedback to maintain profitability and customer satisfaction over time.

4.3: Sourcing quality ingredients and suppliers

Sourcing quality ingredients and establishing reliable supplier relationships are crucial for the success of a food truck business. The freshness and quality of your ingredients directly impact the taste and appeal of your dishes. Here's a detailed guide on how to source quality ingredients and build strong relationships with suppliers:

1. Menu Planning and Ingredient Identification:

- **Menu Development:** Clearly define your menu and the ingredients required for each dish.
- **Ingredient Standards:** Establish standards for the quality, freshness, and source of your ingredients.

2. Local Sourcing:

- **Local Farms and Markets:** Develop relationships with local farmers and markets to source fresh, seasonal produce and other locally produced items.
- **Community Engagement:** Support local businesses and build a positive image by highlighting the use of local ingredients.

3. Quality Standards and Specifications:

- **Supplier Requirements:** Clearly communicate your quality standards and specifications to potential suppliers.
- **Quality Checks:** Regularly inspect and verify the quality of incoming ingredients to ensure they meet your standards.

4. Supplier Research and Selection:

- **Diverse Supplier Network:** Establish relationships with a diverse network of suppliers to ensure a reliable and varied source of ingredients.
- **References and Reviews:** Seek references and reviews from other businesses using the same suppliers.

5. Negotiation and Contracts:

- **Price Negotiation:** Negotiate favorable prices with suppliers without compromising on quality.
- **Contracts:** Establish clear and detailed contracts that outline terms, delivery schedules, and quality expectations.

6. Traceability and Transparency:

- **Supplier Traceability:** Choose suppliers who provide transparency about the origin and sourcing of their products.
- **Certifications:** Prefer suppliers with certifications that demonstrate adherence to food safety and ethical sourcing standards.

7. Communication and Relationship Building:

- **Open Communication:** Foster open communication with suppliers to discuss expectations, changes in menu items, and potential issues.
- **Regular Meetings:** Schedule regular meetings to discuss performance, address concerns, and explore opportunities for collaboration.

8. Consistency and Reliability:

- **Consistent Quality:** Ensure that suppliers consistently deliver ingredients that meet your quality standards.
- **Reliable Delivery:** Work with suppliers who have a track record of reliable and timely deliveries.

9. Inventory Management:

- **Just-in-Time Inventory:** Implement just-in-time inventory management to minimize waste and ensure freshness.
- **Rotation System:** Establish a rotation system for ingredients to use older stock first and minimize the risk of spoilage.

10. Emergency Suppliers:

- **Backup Suppliers:** Identify and establish relationships with backup suppliers to mitigate risks in case of unforeseen circumstances.

- **Emergency Plans:** Have contingency plans for ingredient shortages or disruptions in the supply chain.

11. Seasonal Menu Adaptations:

- **Seasonal Availability:** Adjust your menu based on the seasonal availability of certain ingredients.
- **Collaboration with Suppliers:** Collaborate with suppliers to plan for seasonal changes and ensure a continuous supply of key ingredients.

12. Ethical and Sustainable Sourcing:

- **Ethical Considerations:** Choose suppliers with ethical business practices, fair labor standards, and environmentally sustainable sourcing methods.
- **Certifications:** Seek suppliers with certifications such as organic, fair trade, or sustainable sourcing certifications.

13. Technology Integration:

- **Online Platforms:** Utilize online platforms or software for streamlined communication and ordering processes with suppliers.
- **Digital Tracking:** Implement digital tracking systems to monitor inventory levels and supplier performance.

14. Employee Training:

- **Supplier Relationship Training:** Train staff on the importance of maintaining positive relationships with suppliers and the impact on the overall quality of the food.

15. Feedback and Improvement:

- **Supplier Feedback:** Provide constructive feedback to suppliers to address any issues and improve collaboration.
- **Continuous Improvement:** Encourage continuous improvement in the sourcing process based on customer feedback and changing market trends.

16. Regulatory Compliance:

- **Food Safety Standards:** Ensure that suppliers comply with food safety standards and regulations.

- **Documentation:** Maintain accurate records and documentation of ingredient sourcing to demonstrate compliance during inspections.

Sourcing quality ingredients and building strong supplier relationships is an ongoing process that requires diligence, communication, and adaptability. By prioritizing freshness, transparency, and ethical considerations, your food truck can differentiate itself in the market and provide a superior dining experience for customers. Regularly review and adjust your sourcing strategies to stay competitive and meet the evolving needs of your business.

Chapter 5

Branding and Marketing Strategies

5.1: Building a strong food truck brand

Building a strong food truck brand is essential for success in the competitive mobile food industry. A well-defined and memorable brand helps distinguish your business, creates customer loyalty, and contributes to long-term success. Here's a detailed guide on how to build a strong food truck brand:

1. Define Your Brand Identity:

- **Mission and Values:** Clearly articulate your food truck's mission and values. What does your brand stand for, and what are the principles that guide your business?
- **Unique Selling Proposition (USP):** Identify what makes your food truck unique. This could be a signature dish, a particular cooking technique, or a specific theme.

2. Establish a Unique Brand Name and Logo:

- **Brand Name:** Choose a memorable and easily pronounceable name that reflects your brand identity and concept.

- **Logo Design:** Develop a visually appealing and distinctive logo that communicates the essence of your food truck.

3. Develop a Consistent Visual Identity:

- **Color Palette and Typography:** Choose a consistent color palette and typography for your logo, menu, and overall branding.
- **Graphics and Imagery:** Use high-quality graphics and imagery that align with your brand personality and appeal to your target audience.

4. Craft a Unique Brand Story:

- **Origin Story:** Share the story of how your food truck came into existence. Highlight any unique experiences, challenges overcome, or inspirations behind your brand.
- **Narrative in Marketing:** Weave your brand story into your marketing materials, website, and social media content to create a personal connection with your audience.

5. Consistent Brand Messaging:

- **Tagline:** Develop a catchy and concise tagline that encapsulates your brand message.
- **Voice and Tone:** Establish a consistent voice and tone in your communication, whether it's

on social media, your website, or in-person interactions.

6. Create a Memorable Customer Experience:

- **Friendly Service:** Train your staff to provide excellent customer service and create a positive experience for customers.
- **Engaging Interactions:** Interact with customers in a friendly and engaging manner, reinforcing your brand personality.

7. Optimize Social Media Presence:

- **Consistent Branding Across Platforms:** Maintain consistent branding on all social media platforms, including profile pictures, cover photos, and content.
- **Engagement and Interaction:** Actively engage with your audience through social media by responding to comments, sharing user-generated content, and posting regularly.

8. Create a Professional Website:

- **Mobile-Friendly Design:** Ensure your website is mobile-friendly, considering that many customers may access it on their phones.

- **Menu Presentation:** Showcase your menu with high-quality images and clear descriptions.

9. Leverage Online Reviews and Testimonials:

- **Encourage Reviews:** Encourage satisfied customers to leave positive reviews on platforms like Yelp, Google, or social media.
- **Respond to Feedback:** Respond promptly and professionally to both positive and negative reviews, demonstrating your commitment to customer satisfaction.

10. Participate in Local Events and Collaborations:

- **Community Engagement:** Actively participate in local events, festivals, and collaborations to increase your visibility and build a sense of community around your brand.
- **Sponsorships:** Consider sponsoring local sports teams, community events, or charities to further strengthen your ties with the community.

11. Offer Consistent Quality in Your Products:

- **Menu Consistency:** Ensure consistency in the taste, quality, and presentation of your dishes. This helps build trust among customers.

- **Fresh Ingredients:** Emphasize the use of fresh, high-quality ingredients to reinforce your commitment to providing a superior product.

12. Invest in Professional Brand Photography:

- **High-Quality Imagery:** Invest in professional photography to showcase your food and overall brand in the best light.
- **Visual Storytelling:** Use visuals to tell the story of your brand, from the preparation of dishes to behind-the-scenes moments.

13. Create Merchandise:

- **Branded Merchandise:** Offer branded merchandise, such as T-shirts, hats, or stickers, for customers to purchase. This extends your brand beyond the food and creates additional revenue streams.

14. Monitor and Adapt:

- **Feedback Analysis:** Regularly analyze customer feedback, both online and offline, to understand how your brand is perceived.

- **Adapt to Trends:** Stay informed about industry trends and adapt your branding strategies to remain relevant.

15. Build Partnerships and Collaborations:

- **Collaborate with Other Businesses:** Partner with other local businesses or influencers for joint promotions and collaborations.
- **Cross-Promotions:** Leverage partnerships to cross-promote each other's brands and expand your reach.

16. Consistency Across Touchpoints:

- **Uniformity in Branding:** Ensure a consistent brand experience across all touchpoints, from the food truck's physical appearance to online interactions.
- **Uniform Branding Materials:** Use consistent branding materials such as menus, business cards, and signage.

17. Employee Brand Training:

- **Brand Training Programs:** Train your staff on your brand values, customer service expectations, and the importance of delivering a consistent brand experience.

STARTING A FOOD TRUCK BUSINESS

- **Uniforms and Appearance:** Ensure that your staff's appearance aligns with your brand image.

Building a strong food truck brand is an ongoing process that requires commitment, creativity, and responsiveness to customer feedback. By carefully crafting your brand identity, consistently delivering quality products and experiences, and staying engaged with your community, you can establish a powerful and memorable presence in the competitive food truck industry.

5.2: Leveraging social media for marketing

Leveraging social media for marketing is an integral part of promoting your food truck and building a strong online presence. Social media platforms provide a direct and cost-effective way to engage with your audience, increase brand awareness, and drive customer loyalty. Here's a detailed guide on how to effectively use social media for marketing your food truck:

1. Choose the Right Platforms:

- **Know Your Audience:** Identify the platforms where your target audience is most active. For food-related businesses, platforms like Instagram, Facebook, Twitter, and TikTok are often effective.

- **Platform-Specific Strategies:** Tailor your content and strategies to each platform's unique features and audience demographics.

2. Optimize Profiles for Brand Consistency:

- **Profile Information:** Ensure your profile information, including your bio, location, and contact details, is complete and accurate.
- **Branding Elements:** Use your logo, color scheme, and other branding elements consistently across all your social media profiles.

3. Create Engaging Content:

- **High-Quality Visuals:** Post high-quality and visually appealing photos of your food, the food truck, and behind-the-scenes moments.
- **Video Content:** Incorporate videos, such as cooking demonstrations, behind-the-scenes footage, or customer testimonials, to enhance engagement.
- **Interactive Content:** Encourage interaction with polls, quizzes, and questions to keep your audience engaged.

4. Content Calendar and Consistency:

- **Consistent Posting:** Develop a content calendar to maintain a consistent posting schedule. Regular updates keep your audience interested and engaged.
- **Timing and Frequency:** Analyze when your audience is most active and schedule posts accordingly.

5. Utilize Hashtags Effectively:

- **Branded Hashtags:** Create and promote branded hashtags specific to your food truck. Encourage customers to use them when posting about your food.
- **Trending Hashtags:** Utilize trending and popular hashtags related to the food industry to increase your visibility.

6. Engage with Your Audience:

- **Respond to Comments:** Promptly respond to comments, questions, and messages from your audience. This shows that you value customer interaction.
- **User-Generated Content:** Encourage customers to share photos and experiences with your food truck, and feature user-generated content on your profile.

7. Host Contests and Giveaways:

- **Engagement Boost:** Organize contests or giveaways to boost engagement. Ask followers to tag friends, share posts, or follow your page to participate.
- **Prizes:** Offer appealing prizes, such as free meals or branded merchandise, to incentivize participation.

8. Collaborate with Influencers and Local Businesses:

- **Influencer Marketing:** Partner with local influencers or food bloggers to reach a wider audience and gain credibility.
- **Cross-Promotions:** Collaborate with other local businesses for cross-promotions, helping both parties expand their reach.

9. Showcase Specials and Promotions:

- **Limited-Time Offers:** Announce and promote limited-time specials, discounts, or promotions on social media to create a sense of urgency.
- **Flash Sales:** Use Instagram or Facebook Stories for flash sales or exclusive promotions that disappear after a set period.

10. Utilize Paid Advertising:

- **Targeted Ads:** Use targeted advertising on platforms like Facebook and Instagram to reach specific demographics, locations, or interests.
- **Boosted Posts:** Boost important posts to increase their visibility among your target audience.

11. Share Behind-the-Scenes Content:

- **Kitchen Insights:** Give followers a glimpse into your kitchen, food preparation process, and the people behind the scenes to humanize your brand.
- **Daily Operations:** Share stories about daily operations, from setting up the food truck to closing for the day.

12. Promote Events and Collaborations:

- **Event Announcements:** Use social media to announce your participation in events, festivals, or collaborations.
- **Live Coverage:** Share live updates and coverage from events to build anticipation and provide a real-time connection with your audience.

13. Utilize Social Media Advertising Tools:

- **Analytics:** Leverage analytics tools provided by social media platforms to track the performance of your posts and campaigns.
- **Insights and Metrics:** Monitor metrics like reach, engagement, and audience demographics to refine your social media strategy.

14. Encourage Online Ordering and Reviews:

- **Ordering Information:** Clearly share information about how customers can place orders, whether through a website, third-party delivery apps, or by contacting your food truck directly.
- **Reviews and Testimonials:** Encourage satisfied customers to leave positive reviews on social media platforms and share testimonials.

15. Stay Current with Trends:

- **Stay Informed:** Keep up with current social media trends, algorithm changes, and new features to adapt your strategy accordingly.
- **Adopt New Features:** Explore and adopt new features introduced by social media platforms, such as Stories, Reels, or interactive elements.

16. Monitor Competitors:

- **Competitor Analysis:** Keep an eye on the social media activities of your competitors to identify successful strategies or areas for improvement.
- **Industry Trends:** Stay informed about industry trends by following other food trucks and businesses in the food industry.

17. Analytics and Feedback Analysis:

- **Performance Evaluation:** Regularly analyze analytics and feedback to evaluate the effectiveness of your social media marketing efforts.
- **Adjust Strategies:** Use insights gained from analytics to make data-driven adjustments to your social media strategies.

18. Adapt to Platform Algorithm Changes:

- **Algorithm Understanding:** Stay informed about changes in social media algorithms and adapt your content strategy to maintain visibility.

5.3: Traditional marketing methods for food trucks

While digital marketing and social media have become increasingly popular, traditional marketing methods remain effective for food trucks, especially in reaching local audiences. These methods can help generate awareness, attract customers, and build a loyal customer base. Here's a detailed guide on traditional marketing methods for food trucks:

1. Vehicle Branding and Signage:

- **Eye-Catching Graphics:** Invest in vibrant and eye-catching graphics for your food truck. A well-branded vehicle becomes a moving advertisement.
- **Clear Signage:** Ensure that your menu and contact information are clearly visible on the truck to make it easy for potential customers to learn about your offerings.

2. Flyers and Brochures:

- **Distribution:** Create visually appealing flyers or brochures that showcase your menu, specials, and contact information.
- **Strategic Placement:** Distribute flyers in strategic locations, such as local businesses, community centers, or areas with high foot traffic.

3. Local Print Advertising:

- **Local Newspapers and Magazines:** Advertise your food truck in local newspapers or community magazines.
- **Event Programs:** If you participate in events or festivals, consider placing ads in event programs to reach a targeted audience.

4. Business Cards:

- **Contact Information:** Design and distribute business cards with your food truck's logo, contact information, and social media handles.
- **Handouts with Orders:** Include business cards with every order to encourage repeat business and word-of-mouth referrals.

5. Loyalty Programs and Punch Cards:

- **Rewarding Repeat Business:** Implement a loyalty program that rewards customers for repeat purchases. Consider using punch cards that offer a free item after a certain number of purchases.
- **Visibility on the Truck:** Display information about the loyalty program on the food truck to encourage participation.

6. Partnerships with Local Businesses:

- **Cross-Promotions:** Collaborate with local businesses for cross-promotions. For example, offer discounts to customers who show a receipt from a nearby business.
- **Shared Marketing Materials:** Share marketing materials with partner businesses to expand your reach.

7. Community Sponsorship and Events:

- **Local Events Sponsorship:** Sponsor local events, sports teams, or community organizations. Your logo and food truck presence at these events can boost visibility.
- **Participation in Parades:** Participate in local parades with your food truck, engaging with the community and showcasing your brand.

8. Local Radio Advertising:

- **Radio Spots:** Consider running short radio ads on local stations to reach a broader audience.
- **Event Announcements:** Use radio advertising to announce your participation in upcoming events or festivals.

9. Branded Merchandise:

- **T-Shirts, Hats, and More:** Create and sell branded merchandise such as t-shirts, hats, or reusable bags featuring your food truck's logo.
- **Walking Billboards:** Customers wearing your merchandise become walking billboards, increasing brand visibility.

10. Traditional Signage and Banners:

- **Street-Side Banners:** If your food truck has a regular parking spot, use banners to attract attention from passing pedestrians and motorists.
- **A-Frame Signs:** Place A-frame signs near your truck to announce daily specials, promotions, or menu highlights.

11. Direct Mail Campaigns:

- **Targeted Mailings:** Create targeted direct mail campaigns to reach specific neighborhoods or demographic groups.
- **Coupon Offers:** Include special offers or coupons in the mailings to incentivize first-time customers.

12. Vehicle Location Tracking:

- **Real-Time Updates:** Use social media or a website to provide real-time updates on your food truck's location.
- **Email Notifications:** Allow customers to subscribe to email notifications for location updates and special promotions.

13. Local Community Engagement:

- **Community Events:** Attend local community events, fairs, or markets to engage directly with potential customers.
- **School Partnerships:** Establish partnerships with local schools for catering or special promotions during school events.

14. Local TV Advertising:

- **Cable TV Advertising:** Explore advertising on local cable television channels to reach a wider local audience.
- **Food Features:** If possible, collaborate with local TV channels for featured segments on your food truck and menu.

15. Yellow Pages and Local Directories:

- **Online and Print Listings:** Ensure your food truck is listed in local online directories and print directories like the Yellow Pages.

- **Contact Information:** Provide accurate contact information and a brief description of your food truck in these listings.

16. Billboard Advertising:

- **Strategic Placements:** Consider billboard advertising in high-traffic areas to increase brand visibility.
- **Concise Messaging:** Craft concise and compelling messages that drivers can easily absorb.

17. Vehicle Sound System:

- **Audio Advertisements:** Utilize your food truck's sound system for brief audio advertisements about your specials, promotions, or upcoming events.
- **Musical Atmosphere:** Play music that complements the atmosphere of your food truck, creating a memorable experience for customers.

18. Feedback Collection Mechanisms:

- **Customer Comment Box:** Place a comment box on your food truck to collect feedback from customers.
- **Incentivize Feedback:** Offer small discounts or promotions to customers who provide

feedback, encouraging them to share their thoughts.

19. Testimonials and Reviews:

- **Printed Testimonials:** Showcase positive customer testimonials and reviews on your food truck, website, or marketing materials.
- **Incentivize Reviews:** Encourage customers to leave reviews online by offering discounts or small incentives.

20. Discount Coupons and Mailers:

- **Direct Mail Coupons:** Send out discount coupons or promotional mailers to local households to encourage trial visits.
- **Seasonal Promotions:** Plan seasonal promotions or limited-time offers and promote them through direct mail.

Traditional marketing methods can complement digital strategies, especially when targeting local audiences. The key is to create a well-rounded marketing plan that utilizes both traditional and digital channels to maximize your food truck's reach and impact. Regularly assess the effectiveness of each method and adapt your strategy based on the results.

Chapter 6

Operations and Management

6.1: Staffing and team management

Staffing and team management are critical aspects of running a successful food truck business. A well-managed and motivated team can contribute significantly to the overall customer experience and operational efficiency. Here's a detailed guide on staffing and team management for your food truck:

1. Define Roles and Responsibilities:

- Depending on the size and breadth of your food truck, clearly define the tasks and responsibilities of every team member, including chefs, waiters, cashiers, and any other jobs.
- Ensure that everyone understands their specific duties, helping to streamline operations and avoid confusion.

2. Hiring Process:

- Develop a thorough hiring process that includes screening resumes, conducting interviews, and checking references.
- Look for candidates with relevant experience, a positive attitude, and the ability

to work efficiently in a fast-paced environment.

3. Employee Training:

- Provide comprehensive training for new hires, covering food preparation, safety protocols, customer service standards, and cash handling procedures.
- Conduct ongoing training sessions to keep the team updated on new menu items, promotions, and any changes in processes.

4. Create a Positive Work Environment:

- Foster a positive and inclusive work culture where team members feel valued and motivated.
- Recognize and reward outstanding performance to boost morale and encourage a sense of accomplishment.

5. Communication Channels:

- Establish clear communication channels to ensure that information is effectively conveyed to the entire team.
- Encourage open communication, allowing team members to express concerns or ideas.

6. Scheduling and Shift Management:

- Develop a flexible and fair scheduling system that considers the availability and preferences of your team members.
- Rotate shifts to provide variety and prevent burnout among staff.

7. Performance Feedback:

- Conduct regular performance reviews to provide constructive feedback to team members.
- Recognize achievements and discuss areas for improvement, fostering continuous growth and development.

8. Team Building Activities:

- Plan team-building exercises to help team members get closer. Team-building exercises like team challenges, dinners, and outings can improve cooperation and bonding.

9. Conflict Resolution:

- Establish a clear process for addressing and resolving conflicts within the team.
- Encourage open communication and mediate disputes promptly to maintain a harmonious work environment.

10. Cross-Training:

- Cross-train employees in different roles to enhance flexibility and efficiency.
- This ensures that team members can step into various positions when needed, reducing operational disruptions.

11. Health and Safety Protocols:

- Implement and enforce strict health and safety protocols, especially in the food preparation area.
- Train staff on proper hygiene practices and regularly conduct safety drills.

12. Fair Compensation and Benefits:

- To draw and keep talented workers, provide benefits and pay that are competitive.
- Take into account other benefits like lunch discounts, performance bonuses, or chances for growth.

13. Employee Handbook:

- Develop a comprehensive employee handbook that outlines company policies, expectations, and procedures.
- Provide each team member with a copy and review it during the onboarding process.

14. Uniforms and Appearance Standards:

- Establish clear guidelines for uniforms and appearance standards to maintain a professional and cohesive brand image.
- Ensure that all team members adhere to these standards during working hours.

15. Inventory Management Training:

- Train staff on effective inventory management practices, including tracking stock levels, minimizing waste, and ensuring the freshness of ingredients.
- Empower employees to take ownership of their respective areas, reducing the risk of errors and discrepancies.

16. Customer Service Training:

- Prioritize customer service training to ensure that all team members are well-equipped to provide an excellent customer experience.
- Emphasize the importance of friendliness, attentiveness, and problem-solving skills.

17. Incentive Programs:

- Implement incentive programs, such as performance-based bonuses or recognition programs, to motivate and reward high-performing employees.

- Regularly review and adjust these programs based on team feedback and business objectives.

18. Time-Off and Vacation Policies:

- Establish clear policies regarding time-off requests and vacation scheduling.
- Encourage team members to communicate their availability well in advance, allowing for better planning.

19. Adaptability and Resilience:

- Foster an adaptable and resilient mindset among your team, especially in the face of challenges or unexpected situations.
- Provide training on how to handle peak hours, unexpected rushes, or equipment malfunctions.

20. Continuous Learning Opportunities:

- Encourage continuous learning and professional development by providing opportunities for additional training or workshops.
- Support team members in pursuing certifications or skills enhancement relevant to their roles.

21. Employee Retention Strategies:

- Develop strategies to retain talented employees, including creating a positive work environment, offering advancement opportunities, and recognizing long-term contributions.
- Regularly assess and address factors that may contribute to turnover.

22. Technology Integration:

- Implement technology solutions, such as point-of-sale systems, to streamline order processing and enhance overall efficiency.
- Train staff on the use of technology tools to optimize workflow.

23. Delegation of Responsibilities:

- Delegate responsibilities based on individual strengths and skills.
- Empower team members by entrusting them with specific tasks, fostering a sense of ownership and accountability.

24. Leadership Development:

- Identify and nurture leadership qualities within your team.

- Provide leadership development opportunities, including mentorship programs or leadership training, to prepare employees for future roles.

25. Employee Wellness Programs:

- Consider implementing wellness programs to support the overall well-being of your team.
- This may include mental health resources, wellness challenges, or initiatives that promote a healthy work-life balance.

6.2: Inventory management and ordering

Inventory management and ordering are critical components of running a successful food truck business. Efficiently managing your inventory ensures that you have the right ingredients on hand, minimizes waste, and helps control costs. Here's a detailed guide on inventory management and ordering for your food truck:

1. Establish a Systematic Approach:

- **Inventory Categories:** Categorize your inventory into different groups, such as perishable and non-perishable items, to organize your ordering process.

- **Centralized Storage:** Designate specific areas for storing different types of inventory items to streamline the retrieval process.

2. Implement a POS System:

- **Point-of-Sale (POS) System:** Invest in a POS system that integrates with inventory management. This allows you to track sales and adjust inventory levels automatically.
- **Real-Time Tracking:** Enable real-time tracking of inventory to monitor stock levels and identify popular items.

3. Set Par Levels:

- **Determine Minimum Levels:** Set par levels for each inventory item, indicating the minimum quantity that should be in stock at any given time.
- **Reorder Points:** Establish reorder points to trigger the ordering process when inventory falls below a certain threshold.

4. Regular Physical Counts:

- **Scheduled Counts:** Conduct regular physical counts of your inventory to compare against recorded levels.
- **Spot Checks:** Perform spot checks to verify the accuracy of recorded inventory levels.

5. Vendor Relationships:

- **Build Relationships:** Establish strong relationships with reliable suppliers and vendors.
- **Negotiate Terms:** Negotiate favorable terms, including payment schedules, bulk discounts, and delivery frequencies.

6. Ordering Process:

- **Automate Ordering:** Leverage technology to automate the ordering process, especially for frequently used items.
- **Ordering Calendar:** Develop a regular ordering calendar based on sales patterns and delivery schedules.

7. Forecasting and Seasonal Adjustments:

- **Sales Forecasting:** Analyze historical sales data to forecast future demand accurately.
- **Seasonal Adjustments:** Adjust inventory levels based on seasonal variations and changing customer preferences.

8. First-In-First-Out (FIFO) Method:

- **FIFO Principle:** Implement the FIFO method to ensure that older inventory is used or sold first.

- **Minimize Spoilage:** Minimize the risk of spoilage or expiration by rotating stock according to purchase dates.

9. Technology Integration:

- **Inventory Management Software:** Utilize inventory management software to automate tracking, reorder alerts, and reporting.
- **Cloud-Based Systems:** Consider cloud-based systems for real-time access to inventory data from any location.

10. Monitor Shelf Life and Expiry Dates:

- **Regular Checks:** Regularly check the shelf life and expiration dates of perishable items.
- **Rotate Stock:** Use a first-expiry-first-out (FEFO) approach to minimize waste and ensure freshness.

11. Waste Tracking and Analysis:

- **Track Waste:** Monitor and track waste to identify trends and areas for improvement.
- **Root Cause Analysis:** Conduct root cause analysis for significant waste events and adjust ordering accordingly.

12. Centralized Ordering Authority:

- **Centralized Responsibility:** Designate a central authority or team responsible for inventory management and ordering.
- **Communication Channels:** Establish clear communication channels for inventory needs and adjustments.

13. Bulk Purchasing vs. JIT Inventory:

- **Bulk Purchases:** Consider bulk purchasing for items with longer shelf lives or stable demand.
- **Just-In-Time (JIT):** Use a just-in-time approach for items with shorter shelf lives or variable demand.

14. Supplier Negotiation Skills:

- **Effective Negotiation:** Train staff responsible for ordering on effective negotiation skills.
- **Leverage Relationships:** Leverage strong supplier relationships for better terms and pricing.

15. Emergency Ordering Protocols:

- **Emergency Contacts:** Establish emergency contacts with suppliers for urgent orders or unforeseen circumstances.

- **Backup Suppliers:** Identify backup suppliers to mitigate risks in case of disruptions with primary suppliers.

16. Use Historical Data for Trends:

- **Sales Patterns:** Analyze historical sales data to identify trends and adjust ordering accordingly.
- **Seasonal Adjustments:** Make informed decisions based on seasonal variations and customer preferences.

17. Document and Analyze:

- **Record Keeping:** Maintain detailed records of all inventory transactions, including deliveries, consumption, and waste.
- **Regular Analysis:** Regularly analyze inventory data to identify areas for improvement and cost-saving opportunities.

18. Employee Training:

- **Inventory Training:** Train staff on proper inventory management procedures, including accurate recording, storage practices, and order requisition processes.
- **Cross-Training:** Cross-train employees to handle multiple roles within inventory management, ensuring flexibility in staffing.

19. Regular Supplier Reviews:

- **Performance Evaluation:** Regularly evaluate supplier performance in terms of reliability, quality, and adherence to agreed-upon terms.
- **Feedback and Adjustments:** Provide constructive feedback to suppliers and adjust your ordering strategy based on their performance.

20. Adaptability and Continuous Improvement:

- **Adapt to Changes:** Stay flexible and adapt your inventory management strategy based on changing market conditions, customer preferences, and business growth.
- **Continuous Improvement:** Encourage a culture of continuous improvement, where the team actively seeks ways to enhance efficiency and reduce costs.

21. Integrate Sustainability Practices:

- **Reduce Packaging Waste:** Work with suppliers who prioritize eco-friendly packaging to minimize environmental impact.
- **Donate Surplus Food:** Establish partnerships with local charities or organizations to donate surplus food,

minimizing waste and contributing to community initiatives.

22. Regular Equipment Maintenance:

- **Refrigeration and Storage Equipment:** Regularly maintain and service refrigeration and storage equipment to prevent breakdowns that could lead to inventory spoilage.
- **Temperature Monitoring:** Implement systems to monitor and record storage temperatures to ensure food safety.

23. Budgeting and Cost Control:

- **Cost Analysis:** Conduct regular cost analyses to identify areas where costs can be controlled or reduced.
- **Budget Planning:** Develop a budget for your inventory and track expenses to stay within financial targets.

24. Document Standard Operating Procedures (SOPs):

- **Create SOPs:** Document standard operating procedures for all aspects of inventory management, including ordering, receiving, storing, and tracking.

- **Training Material:** Use SOPs as training material for new hires and a reference guide for existing staff.

25. Regular Audits:

- **Internal Audits:** Conduct internal audits of your inventory management processes to identify any discrepancies or areas for improvement.
- **External Audits:** Consider external audits to gain an unbiased assessment of your inventory management practices.

26. Communication with Front-of-House:

- **Collaboration:** Foster communication between the back-of-house and front-of-house teams to align inventory needs with customer demand.
- **Feedback Loop:** Establish a feedback loop to share customer preferences and menu adjustments that may impact inventory requirements.

6.3: Point-of-sale systems and technology integration

Point-of-sale (POS) systems and technology integration play a crucial role in enhancing the efficiency, accuracy, and overall success of a food truck business. A well-implemented POS system goes beyond simply processing transactions; it streamlines operations, provides valuable insights, and improves the overall customer experience. Here's a detailed guide on the importance and implementation of POS systems and technology integration for food trucks:

1. Importance of POS Systems:

- **Transaction Processing:** The primary function of a POS system is to facilitate transactions quickly and accurately.
- **Inventory Management:** Many modern POS systems integrate with inventory management, helping to track stock levels and reduce the risk of overstock or stockouts.
- **Sales Reporting:** POS systems generate detailed sales reports, allowing business owners to analyze performance, identify trends, and make informed decisions.

2. Features of Advanced POS Systems:

- **Order Customization:** Advanced POS systems allow for easy customization of orders, accommodating customer preferences and dietary restrictions.

- **Employee Management:** This feature is available in certain POS systems features, including clock-in/out capabilities and performance tracking.
- **Customer Relationship Management (CRM):** CRM features help build and maintain customer relationships by tracking purchase history and preferences.

3. Mobile POS Solutions:

- **Tablet or Smartphone Integration:** Mobile POS solutions allow food trucks to use tablets or smartphones for transactions, providing flexibility in serving customers at different locations.
- **Ordering Efficiency:** Mobile POS systems enable staff to take orders directly from customers in line, reducing wait times and improving overall efficiency.

4. Cloud-Based POS Systems:

- **Remote Access:** Cloud-based POS systems provide remote access to sales data, allowing business owners to monitor operations from anywhere.
- **Data Security:** Cloud-based systems often have robust security measures, protecting sensitive customer and business information.

5. Ordering Kiosks:

- **Self-Service Options:** Implementing ordering kiosks or tablets allows customers to place their orders directly, reducing wait times and enhancing the overall customer experience.
- **Integration with POS:** Ensure that kiosks seamlessly integrate with your POS system to maintain a unified order processing flow.

6. Contactless Payments:

- **Tap and Go Technology:** Implement contactless payment options, such as NFC (Near Field Communication) technology, to accommodate customers who prefer quick and secure payment methods.
- **Mobile Wallet Integration:** Enable payments through popular mobile wallets like Apple Pay, Google Pay, or other contactless options.

7. Integration with Online Ordering Platforms:

- **Third-Party Integration:** Integrate your POS system with popular online ordering platforms to streamline the processing of online orders.
- **Menu Synchronization:** Ensure that your online and on-site menus are synchronized to

avoid discrepancies and maintain consistency.

8. Inventory Management Integration:

- **Real-Time Tracking:** POS systems with integrated inventory management provide real-time tracking of stock levels.
- **Automated Alerts:** Set up automated alerts for low stock levels, helping to prevent stockouts and optimize ordering processes.

9. Analytics and Reporting:

- **Sales Analytics:** POS systems offer detailed analytics and reporting tools, allowing businesses to analyze sales patterns, identify top-selling items, and make data-driven decisions.
- **Customer Insights:** Gain insights into customer behavior, preferences, and peak ordering times to tailor marketing efforts and menu offerings.

10. Menu Management:

- **Dynamic Menu Updates:** Easily update and modify your menu on the POS system to accommodate changes in offerings, seasonal items, or pricing adjustments.

- **Visual Displays:** Some POS systems support visual displays of the menu, helping customers make informed choices.

11. Integration with Loyalty Programs:

- **Automated Reward Tracking:** Link your POS system to a loyalty program to automatically track customer purchases and reward them for their loyalty.
- **Promotional Campaigns:** Use POS data to design targeted promotional campaigns for loyal customers.

12. Employee Access Controls:

- **Role-Based Access:** Put in place role-based access controls to guarantee that workers can only access the data and functionality required for their jobs.
- **Security Measures:** Secure the POS system with passwords and implement additional security measures to protect against unauthorized access.

13. Seamless Offline Functionality:

- **Offline Transaction Support:** Make that the point-of-sale system can continue to process transactions in an offline mode, enabling the company to function even in places with spotty internet access.

- **Automatic Syncing:** Implement automatic syncing when the POS system regains internet access to update transaction data.

14. Hardware Compatibility:

- **Choose Compatible Hardware:** Ensure that your chosen POS system is compatible with the hardware you have or plan to use, including receipt printers, cash registers, and card readers.
- **Scalability:** Opt for a scalable POS solution that can accommodate the growth of your food truck business.

15. Training and Support:

- **Comprehensive Training:** Provide thorough training for your staff on how to use the POS system effectively, covering order processing, payment handling, and basic troubleshooting.
- **Vendor Support:** Choose a POS provider that offers reliable customer support and assistance, especially during the initial setup and any troubleshooting scenarios.

16. Regular Updates and Maintenance:

- **Software Updates:** Keep the POS software up-to-date with the latest releases to access new features, improvements, and security patches.
- **Routine Maintenance:** Schedule routine maintenance checks for both hardware and software components to identify and address potential issues promptly.

17. User-Friendly Interface:

- **Intuitive Design:** Select a POS system with an intuitive and user-friendly interface to minimize training time for new staff members.
- **Touchscreen Capabilities:** If using a touchscreen, ensure that it is responsive and easy to navigate for both staff and customers.

18. Compliance with Regulations:

- **Payment Card Industry Data Security Standard (PCI DSS):** Ensure that your POS system complies with PCI DSS to protect customer payment information.
- **Data Privacy Regulations:** Stay informed about and comply with data privacy regulations applicable to your location.

19. Budget Considerations:

- **Total Cost of Ownership:** Consider the total cost of ownership, including hardware, software, maintenance, and any additional fees associated with the POS system.
- **Return on Investment (ROI):** Evaluate the potential ROI based on increased efficiency, reduced errors, and improved customer satisfaction.

20. Adaptability to Emerging Technologies:

- **Future-Proofing:** Select a POS system that can adapt to emerging technologies and industry trends, ensuring that your business remains competitive in the long run.
- **Integration with New Features:** Periodically review your POS system to integrate new features or technologies that enhance your food truck operations.

A well-chosen POS system and effective technology integration contribute significantly to the success of a food truck business. The right technology not only streamlines day-to-day operations but also provides valuable data and insights that can be leveraged for business growth and customer satisfaction. Regularly assess your POS system's performance, stay informed about technological advancements, and adapt your technology strategy to meet the evolving needs of your food truck business.

Chapter 7

Financial Management

7.1: Budgeting and financial planning

Budgeting and financial planning are essential components of managing a successful food truck business. A well-structured budget not only helps you allocate resources efficiently but also serves as a roadmap for achieving financial goals and sustaining profitability. Here's a detailed guide on budgeting and financial planning for your food truck:

1. Create a Comprehensive Business Plan:

- **Executive Summary:** Provide a concise overview of your food truck business, including your mission, vision, and key objectives.
- **Market Analysis:** Conduct thorough market research to understand your target audience, competitors, and industry trends.
- **Financial Projections:** Include detailed financial projections, outlining expected expenses, revenue forecasts, and profitability estimates.

2. Start with a Sales Forecast:

- **Research and Analysis:** Estimate your expected sales based on market research, historical data (if available), and your unique value proposition.
- **Break Down by Product/Service:** Break down sales forecasts by product or service categories to identify top-performing items and allocate resources accordingly.

3. Fixed and Variable Costs:

- **Fixed Costs:** Identify fixed costs, such as permits, licenses, insurance, and lease payments, that remain consistent regardless of sales volume.
- **Variable Costs:** Variable costs, like ingredients, fuel, and labor, fluctuate with the level of sales. Categorize and estimate these costs based on your sales forecast.

4. Operating Expenses:

- **Daily Operations:** Factor in day-to-day operational expenses, including fuel, maintenance, and restocking, to ensure accurate budgeting.
- **Marketing and Promotion:** Allocate a portion of your budget for marketing and promotional activities to attract and retain customers.

5. Employee Wages and Benefits:

- **Labor Costs:** Indicate in detail the pay scale for all of your employees, including servers, cooks, and other staff members. Take into account both prospective overtime expenses and hourly wages.
- **Benefits and Taxes:** Factor in additional costs such as benefits, payroll taxes, and workers' compensation.

6. Equipment and Maintenance:

- **Initial Costs:** Add the price of buying or renting the food truck, the cost of the kitchen appliances, and any other gear needed for regular operations.
- **Maintenance and Repairs:** Budget for ongoing maintenance and repairs to ensure the longevity of your equipment.

7. Licenses and Permits:

- **Research Fees:** Research and estimate the costs associated with obtaining necessary licenses and permits, including health permits, parking permits, and business licenses.
- **Renewal Costs:** Consider the renewal fees for licenses and permits that may need to be paid annually.

8. Insurance:

- **Liability Insurance:** Obtain liability insurance to protect your business from potential legal claims. Include insurance premiums in your budget.
- **Vehicle Insurance:** Budget for insurance coverage specific to your food truck, covering both the vehicle and its contents.

9. Taxes:

- **Income Taxes:** Estimate your income tax obligations based on your projected profits. Seek advice from a tax expert to guarantee correctness.
- **Sales Taxes:** If they apply, account for them and schedule monthly payments to the relevant tax authorities.

10. Contingency Fund:

- **Emergency Fund:** Allocate a portion of your budget to an emergency fund or contingency reserve to cover unexpected expenses or downturns in business.
- **Risk Mitigation:** Anticipate potential risks and plan for how your business would navigate unforeseen challenges.

11. Debt Servicing:

- **Loan Payments:** If you have taken loans to start or grow your food truck business, budget for regular loan payments.
- **Interest Costs:** Include interest costs associated with loans in your budget.

12. Profit Margin Analysis:

- **Calculate Profit Margins:** Regularly analyze your profit margins to assess the financial health of your business.
- **Identify Cost Drivers:** Identify and manage factors that impact your profit margins, such as ingredient costs, operating expenses, and pricing strategies.

13. Cash Flow Management:

- **Track Inflows and Outflows:** Track Inflows and Outflows: Maintain a detailed cash flow statement that tracks the inflows and outflows of cash.
- Payment Terms: Negotiate favorable payment terms with suppliers to optimize cash flow.

14. Financial Software and Tools:

- **Use Accounting Software:** Implement accounting software to streamline financial processes, track expenses, and generate accurate financial reports.

- **Budgeting Apps:** Utilize budgeting apps that provide real-time insights into your financial performance and help you stay on track.

15. Review and Adjust Regularly:

- **Monthly Reviews:** Conduct monthly reviews of your budget against actual performance to identify any variances.
- **Adjust as Needed:** Adjust your budget based on changing circumstances, market conditions, or unexpected events.

16. Investment in Marketing and Branding:

- **Allocate Marketing Budget:** Dedicate a portion of your budget to marketing efforts, such as social media advertising, local events, and promotions.
- **Branding Initiatives:** Invest in branding initiatives that differentiate your food truck and attract a loyal customer base.

17. Negotiate with Suppliers:

- **Bulk Discounts:** Negotiate bulk discounts with suppliers to reduce ingredient costs.
- **Payment Terms:** Negotiate favorable payment terms, such as extended payment periods or early payment discounts.

18. Financial Forecasting:

- **Long-Term Projections:** Extend your financial forecasting beyond the immediate future to identify potential growth opportunities or challenges.
- **Scenario Analysis:** Conduct scenario analysis to assess the impact of different market conditions on your financial performance.

19. Savings for Expansion or Upgrades:

- **Future Growth:** Allocate funds for future expansion or upgrades, such as acquiring additional food trucks, expanding the menu, or entering new markets.
- **Research and Development:** Invest in research and development for menu innovation and staying ahead of industry trends.

20. Educate and Involve Your Team:

- **Staff Training:** Educate your staff about the importance of budgeting and cost control, instilling a sense of financial responsibility.
- **Open Communication:** Foster open communication with your team, encouraging them to provide insights or suggestions for cost-saving measures.

21. Government Assistance and Grants:

- **Explore Opportunities:** Research government assistance programs or grants available to small businesses in the food industry.
- **Eligibility Criteria:** Understand the eligibility criteria and application processes for any available financial support.

22. Benchmarking Against Industry Standards:

- **Industry Comparisons:** Benchmark your financial performance against industry standards to identify areas for improvement.
- **Networking:** Engage with other food truck owners or industry professionals to gain insights and share best practices.

23. Customer Feedback and Adaptability:

- **Feedback Mechanisms:** Use customer feedback to make informed decisions about menu adjustments, pricing, and overall customer satisfaction.
- **Adapt to Market Changes:** Stay adaptable to changes in customer preferences, market trends, and economic conditions.

24. Professional Financial Advice:

- **Consult Financial Advisors:** Seek advice from financial advisors or accountants to ensure your budget aligns with your business goals and industry best practices.
- **Tax Planning:** Work with professionals to develop tax planning strategies that optimize your financial position.

25. Maintain a Disciplined Approach:

- **Stick to the Budget:** Adhere to your budget and financial plan, avoiding unnecessary expenses or deviations that can impact profitability.
- **Regular Reassessments:** Regularly reassess your financial plan to ensure it aligns with your evolving business goals.

Effective budgeting and financial planning are ongoing processes that require diligence and adaptability. By carefully managing your resources, controlling costs, and making strategic financial decisions, you can position your food truck business for long-term success and sustainability in a competitive market. Regularly revisit and update your budget to reflect changing circumstances and seize opportunities for growth and efficiency.

7.2: Pricing for profit and cost control

Pricing for profit and cost control are integral aspects of managing a successful food truck business. Establishing the right pricing strategy ensures that your business is profitable, covering costs while providing value to customers. Here's a detailed guide on pricing for profit and effective cost control:

1. Understand Cost Structures:

- **Fixed Costs:** Identify fixed costs that remain constant regardless of sales volume, such as permits, licenses, and insurance.
- **Variable Costs:** Recognize variable costs that fluctuate with sales, including ingredients, fuel, and labor.

2. Calculate Cost of Goods Sold (COGS):

- **Ingredient Costs:** Determine the cost of ingredients per dish to calculate the COGS.
- **Recipe Analysis:** Conduct a thorough analysis of recipes to understand the contribution of each ingredient to the overall cost.

3. Determine Desired Profit Margin:

- **Profit Goals:** Set clear profit goals based on your business objectives, financial projections, and industry standards.

- **Percentage Margin:** Decide on a target profit margin percentage that aligns with your business strategy.

4. Competitor Analysis:

- **Study Competitor Pricing:** Analyze the pricing strategies of competitors in your market.
- **Value Comparison:** Assess the perceived value of your offerings compared to competitors, considering factors like quality, portion size, and uniqueness.

5. Customer Perception and Market Positioning:

- **Perceived Value:** Understand how customers perceive the value of your food and the experience you provide.
- **Market Positioning:** Position your food truck in the market based on factors like quality, innovation, or affordability.

6. Markup Pricing vs. Cost-Plus Pricing:

- **Markup Pricing:** Determine the desired profit margin and apply a markup percentage to the cost to establish the selling price.
- **Cost-Plus Pricing:** Add a predetermined profit amount to the total cost to set the selling price.

7. Tiered Pricing or Bundle Offers:

- **Tiered Pricing:** Offer different pricing tiers for various menu items based on factors like size, complexity, or premium ingredients.
- **Bundle Offers:** Create bundled deals or combo offers to encourage customers to purchase multiple items.

8. Dynamic Pricing Strategies:

- **Time-Based Pricing:** Implement time-based pricing, adjusting prices during peak hours or special events.
- **Seasonal Pricing:** Consider seasonal pricing adjustments to account for changes in demand or ingredient costs.

9. Value-Based Pricing:

- **Customer Perception:** Determine the perceived value of your offerings and set prices accordingly.
- **Unique Selling Proposition (USP):** Highlight unique features or qualities that justify higher prices.

10. Evaluate and Adjust Pricing Regularly:

- **Regular Reviews:** Conduct regular reviews of your pricing strategy, considering factors like ingredient costs, competitor pricing, and customer feedback.
- **Adapt to Market Changes:** Be adaptable to market changes, adjusting prices as needed to remain competitive and profitable.

11. Economies of Scale:

- **Bulk Purchasing:** Leverage economies of scale by negotiating bulk discounts with suppliers for high-volume ingredient purchases.
- **Operational Efficiency:** Streamline operations to increase efficiency, reducing per-unit costs as sales volume grows.

12. Cost Control Measures:

- **Inventory Management:** Implement efficient inventory management practices to minimize waste and control ingredient costs.
- **Operational Efficiency:** Streamline processes and workflows to reduce labor costs and improve overall efficiency.

13. Pricing Psychology:

- **Charm Pricing:** Consider charm pricing by setting prices just below whole numbers (e.g.,

$4.99 instead of $5.00) to create a perception of lower prices.

- **Pricing Anchoring:** Display higher-priced items alongside lower-priced items to make the latter seem more affordable.

14. Menu Engineering:

- **Highlight Profitable Items:** Strategically place high-profit-margin items on the menu to attract attention.
- **Promote Best Sellers:** Promote best-selling items to drive sales and maximize revenue.

15. Loyalty Programs and Discounts:

- **Customer Retention:** Implement loyalty programs to encourage repeat business and reward loyal customers.
- **Strategic Discounts:** Offer targeted discounts during slow periods or on specific menu items to boost sales.

16. Cost Tracking and Analysis:

- **Regular Cost Reviews:** Conduct regular reviews of all costs, including ingredients, labor, and operational expenses.
- **Identify Cost Variations:** Identify any cost variations and take corrective action to maintain profitability.

17. Supplier Negotiations:

- **Negotiate Favorable Terms:** Negotiate favorable terms with suppliers, such as bulk discounts, payment schedules, or exclusivity arrangements.
- **Explore Multiple Suppliers:** Consider working with multiple suppliers to compare costs and maintain flexibility.

18. Technology Integration for Efficiency:

- **POS System Integration:** Integrate your POS system with inventory management to track sales and ingredient usage in real-time.
- **Automated Ordering:** Use technology to automate the ordering process, reducing the risk of overstock or stockouts.

19. Customer Feedback and Data Analysis:

- **Customer Surveys:** Gather feedback from customers on pricing, portion sizes, and overall value.
- **Data Analytics:** Analyze sales data to identify customer preferences and adjust pricing or menu offerings accordingly.

20. Training and Empowering Staff:

- **Cost-Conscious Culture:** Train staff on the importance of cost control and maintaining profitability.
- **Empowerment:** Empower staff to suggest cost-saving measures or improvements in operational efficiency.

21. Explore Alternative Ingredients or Suppliers:

- **Ingredient Substitutions:** Consider alternative, cost-effective ingredients without compromising quality.
- **Supplier Comparison:** Explore different suppliers to find the most cost-efficient options without sacrificing quality.

22. Manage Portion Sizes:

- **Cost-Effective Portions:** Find a balance between offering generous portions and controlling ingredient costs.
- **Value Perception:** Ensure that portion sizes align with customer expectations and the perceived value of your offerings.

23. Government Regulations and Compliance:

- **Pricing Transparency:** Ensure compliance with pricing transparency regulations to build trust with customers.

- **Tax Considerations:** Account for applicable taxes in your pricing strategy to avoid surprises.

24. Promotions and Limited-Time Offers:

- **Strategic Promotions:** Plan promotions and limited-time offers to drive sales and create a sense of urgency.
- **Bundle Deals:** Introduce bundled deals or special packages to encourage upselling and increase average transaction value.

25. Educate Customers on Value:

- **Communicate Value Proposition:** Clearly communicate the value proposition of your food truck, emphasizing quality, freshness, and uniqueness.
- **Transparency:** Be transparent about your pricing, helping customers understand the reasons behind your prices.

26. Risk Management:

- **Mitigate External Risks:** Anticipate external factors that could impact costs, such as fluctuations in ingredient prices or changes in regulations.
- **Contingency Planning:** Develop contingency plans to navigate unexpected

challenges without compromising profitability.

27. Benchmarking and Industry Analysis:

- **Benchmark Against Competitors:** Regularly benchmark your pricing against competitors to ensure competitiveness.
- **Industry Trends:** Stay informed about industry trends that may impact pricing strategies and adjust accordingly.

28. Ethical Considerations:

- **Fair Pricing:** Strive for fair pricing that reflects the value you provide while considering the economic realities of your target market.
- **Transparent Practices:** Maintain transparent pricing practices to build trust with customers.

29. Regular Profit and Loss Analysis:

- **Review Financial Statements:** Regularly review profit and loss statements to assess overall business performance.
- **Identify Opportunities:** Identify opportunities for cost savings, pricing adjustments, or revenue growth.

30. Invest in Continuous Improvement:

- **Feedback Loop:** Establish a feedback loop with customers, staff, and suppliers to gather insights for continuous improvement.
- **Adaptability:** Stay adaptable to market changes, incorporating lessons learned and making data-driven adjustments to your pricing strategy.

In conclusion, pricing for profit and cost control require a strategic approach that considers various factors, including costs, market dynamics, and customer perceptions. Regularly reassess and refine your pricing strategy to align with your business goals, remain competitive, and sustain profitability over the long term. The ability to balance customer value with operational efficiency is key to establishing a successful and sustainable pricing model for your food truck business.

7.3: Tax considerations for food trucks

Tax considerations are a crucial aspect of running a food truck business, and understanding the tax obligations and opportunities is essential for maintaining financial health and compliance. Here's a detailed guide on tax considerations for food trucks:

1. Business Structure:

- **Sole Proprietorship, Partnership, LLC, or Corporation:** Choose the appropriate business structure, each with its own tax implications.
- **Consultation with a Tax Professional:** Seek advice from a tax professional to determine the most tax-efficient structure for your specific situation.

2. Employment Taxes:

- **Social Security and Medicare Taxes:** As an employer, you are responsible for withholding and paying Social Security and Medicare taxes on behalf of your employees.
- **Federal Income Tax Withholding:** Withhold federal income tax from employees' wages based on their Form W-4.

3. Self-Employment Tax:

- **Owner's Responsibility:** Business owners in a sole proprietorship or single-member LLC are generally responsible for self-employment taxes.
- **Estimated Quarterly Payments:** Pay estimated taxes quarterly to cover income and self-employment tax liabilities.

4. Sales Tax:

- **Sales Tax Registration:** Register for a sales tax permit with the appropriate state and local tax authorities.
- **Collection and Remittance:** Collect and remit sales tax on taxable sales. Rates and rules vary by jurisdiction.

5. Income Tax:

- **Recordkeeping:** Maintain detailed records of income and expenses for accurate income tax reporting.
- **Tax Deductions:** Identify eligible business expenses for tax deductions, including costs associated with food, fuel, maintenance, and equipment.

6. Tax Deductions for Food Trucks:

- **Cost of Goods Sold (COGS):** Deduct the cost of ingredients, packaging, and other directly related costs in calculating COGS.
- **Operating Expenses:** Deduct operating expenses such as vehicle maintenance, insurance, licenses, permits, and marketing costs.

7. Depreciation:

- **Depreciation Deduction:** Depreciate the cost of assets (e.g., the food truck itself, kitchen equipment) over their useful lives to claim tax deductions.
- **Section 179 Deduction:** Take advantage of Section 179 for immediate expensing of certain qualifying assets.

8. Meals and Entertainment Deductions:

- **Business Meals Deduction:** Deduct a percentage of business meal expenses, including meals provided for employees or at business meetings.
- **Recordkeeping:** Keep detailed records, including receipts and notes on the business purpose of meals and entertainment expenses.

9. Home Office Deduction:

- **Qualification Criteria:** If you use a home office for administrative tasks, you may be eligible for a home office deduction.
- **Proportional Allocation:** Deduct a portion of home-related expenses, such as rent, utilities, and insurance, based on the percentage of your home used for business.

10. Vehicle Expenses:

- **Standard Mileage Rate or Actual Expenses:** Choose between the standard mileage rate or actual expenses (including fuel, maintenance, and depreciation) for deducting vehicle costs.
- **Recordkeeping:** Maintain a mileage log and keep receipts for actual expenses.

11. Tax Credits:

- **Research and Development (R&D) Credits:** Investigate whether your business activities qualify for R&D credits, which can offset tax liabilities.
- **Work Opportunity Tax Credit (WOTC):** If applicable, take advantage of WOTC for hiring individuals from certain targeted groups.

12. Health Insurance Deduction:

- **Self-Employed Health Insurance Deduction:** Deduct the cost of health insurance premiums for yourself, your spouse, and dependents.
- **Eligibility Criteria:** Ensure you meet the eligibility criteria for the self-employed health insurance deduction.

13. Retirement Plans:

- **SEP-IRA or SIMPLE IRA:** Consider setting up a Simplified Employee Pension (SEP) IRA or Savings Incentive Match Plan for Employees (SIMPLE) IRA for potential tax advantages.
- **Employee Contributions:** Encourage employee participation in retirement plans to benefit from tax-deferred savings.

14. State and Local Taxes:

- **State Income Tax:** Understand your state's income tax regulations and comply with filing requirements.
- **Local Taxes:** Be aware of any additional local taxes that may apply to your food truck business.

15. Tax Compliance Calendar:

- **Important Deadlines:** Stay organized with a tax compliance calendar that includes key deadlines for filing various tax forms and making payments.
- **Quarterly Estimated Taxes:** Plan for and make quarterly estimated tax payments to avoid penalties.

16. Tax Professional Consultation:

- **Regular Consultation:** Schedule regular consultations with a tax professional to stay informed about changes in tax laws and regulations.
- **Strategic Tax Planning:** Seek advice on strategic tax planning to optimize your business's financial position.

17. Tax Reporting for Employees:

- **W-2 Forms:** Provide employees with W-2 forms by the designated deadline, summarizing their annual wages and tax withholdings.
- **Payroll Tax Returns:** File quarterly and annual payroll tax returns, including Form 941 and Form 940.

18. Tax Withholding for Employees:

- **Form W-4:** Have employees complete Form W-4 to determine the appropriate amount of federal income tax to withhold.
- **State Withholding:** Comply with state withholding requirements for income tax.

19. Tax Incentives for Eco-Friendly Practices:

- **Energy-Efficient Equipment:** Take advantage of tax incentives for using energy-efficient equipment in your food truck.

- **Renewable Energy Credits:** Explore opportunities for renewable energy credits related to your business operations.

20. Disaster and COVID-19 Relief Provisions:

- **Research Relief Measures:** Stay informed about disaster relief measures and tax provisions related to events like natural disasters or pandemics.
- **Claiming Tax Credits:** Explore any available tax credits or relief provisions introduced in response to crises.

21. Understanding Tax Changes:

- **Stay Updated:** Regularly review tax publications, updates, and changes to ensure compliance with the latest regulations.
- **Adapt to Changes:** Adapt your tax strategy as needed based on changes in tax laws and regulations.

22. Recordkeeping Practices:

- **Organized Records:** Keep organized records of all financial transactions, receipts, and tax-related documents.
- **Digital Recordkeeping:** Consider digital recordkeeping solutions for ease of retrieval and to minimize the risk of document loss.

23. Tax Liability Planning:

- **Proactive Planning:** Proactively plan for tax liabilities to avoid surprises and ensure funds are set aside for tax payments.
- **Tax Planning Sessions:** Schedule regular tax planning sessions to assess your business's financial position and identify opportunities for tax savings.

24. Tax Credits for Employee Training:

- **Employment Credits:** Explore tax credits available for employee training programs or certifications that enhance workforce skills.
- **Document Training Expenses:** Maintain documentation of training expenses for potential tax credits.

25. Understanding Deductible vs. Non-Deductible Expenses:

- **Professional Guidance:** Seek professional guidance to distinguish between deductible and non-deductible expenses.
- **Tax-Advantageous Spending:** Understand how certain spending decisions may have tax implications, whether favorable or not.

26. Tax-Favored Retirement Contributions:

- **Contributions to Retirement Accounts:** Maximize contributions to tax-favored retirement accounts to reduce taxable income.
- **Educate Employees:** Educate employees about the benefits of contributing to retirement accounts.

27. Tax Implications of Expansion:

- **Consultation for Expansion Plans:** If expanding to new locations or markets, consult with tax professionals to understand the tax implications.
- **State Nexus Considerations:** Be aware of state nexus rules that may affect tax obligations in additional locations.

28. Foreign Income and Tax Implications:

- **International Operations:** If your food truck operates internationally, understand the tax implications of foreign income and transactions.
- **Cross-Border Tax Compliance:** Comply with cross-border tax regulations and seek guidance on any applicable tax treaties.

29. Review of Tax Credits and Incentives:

- **Regular Review:** Regularly review available tax credits and incentives at the federal, state, and local levels.
- **Applicability Assessment:** Assess the applicability of tax credits and incentives to your food truck business activities.

30. Educate Staff on Tax Compliance:

- **Staff Training:** Educate staff, especially those involved in financial recordkeeping, on tax compliance requirements.
- **Importance of Accuracy:** Emphasize the importance of accurate reporting and compliance to avoid potential penalties.

Navigating the complexities of tax considerations for a food truck business requires careful planning, continuous education, and collaboration with tax professionals. Staying informed about tax regulations, strategically planning for tax liabilities, and maintaining meticulous recordkeeping are critical components of a successful tax strategy. Regularly reassess your tax position in light of changing circumstances and leverage available tax incentives to optimize your food truck business's financial performance.

Chapter 8

Growing Your Food Truck Business

8.1: Expanding to new locations and events

Expanding your food truck business to new locations and events is an exciting opportunity for growth and increased revenue. However, it requires careful planning, strategic decision-making, and effective execution to ensure a successful expansion. Here's a detailed guide on how to navigate the process of expanding your food truck to new locations and events:

1. Market Research and Analysis:

- **Target Audience:** Identify the target audience in the new locations or events. Understand their preferences, tastes, and spending habits.
- **Competition Analysis:** Research existing food options in the area to identify gaps in the market and determine how your food truck can stand out.

2. Legal and Regulatory Compliance:

- **Permits and Licenses:** Research and obtain all necessary permits and licenses for operating in the new locations. Compliance with health codes, zoning regulations, and other local laws is crucial.

- **Insurance Coverage:** Ensure that your insurance coverage is sufficient for the new locations and events, covering potential risks and liabilities.

3. Logistics and Infrastructure:

- **Vehicle Readiness:** Assess whether your food truck is equipped for the specific needs of the new locations or events. Consider any necessary modifications or additions.
- **Storage and Supply Chain:** Establish efficient logistics for sourcing ingredients, storing supplies, and managing inventory in the new locations.

4. Financial Planning:

- **Budgeting for Expansion:** Develop a comprehensive budget for the expansion, considering costs such as permits, marketing, staff, and operational expenses.
- **Financial Projections:** Create realistic financial projections to estimate potential revenue and expenses in the new locations.

5. Marketing and Branding:

- **Localized Marketing Strategies:** Develop marketing strategies tailored to the new locations. Utilize local media, social media, and community engagement to build awareness.
- **Branding Consistency:** Ensure that your food truck maintains a consistent brand image across all locations. Adapt marketing materials to suit the local context.

6. Menu Adaptation:

- **Local Tastes and Preferences:** Modify your menu to cater to the tastes and preferences of the local population.
- **Seasonal Offerings:** Consider incorporating seasonal or regional specialties to attract and appeal to the local customer base.

7. Staffing and Training:

- **Hiring Considerations:** Assess whether additional staff is needed for the expansion. Hire personnel familiar with the local area to enhance customer interactions.
- **Training Programs:** Implement training programs to ensure that staff members understand the nuances of operating in new locations and delivering consistent service.

8. Collaborations and Partnerships:

- **Local Partnerships:** Explore collaborations with local businesses, event organizers, or community groups to enhance your presence in the new locations.
- **Cross-Promotions:** Partner with other vendors or businesses for cross-promotional opportunities that benefit both parties.

9. Technology Integration:

- **POS Systems:** Ensure that your Point of Sale (POS) system is adaptable to different locations and events. Consider cloud-based systems for flexibility.
- **Mobile Ordering Apps:** Implement mobile ordering apps to streamline the ordering process, especially in busy event settings.

10. Customer Engagement and Feedback:

- **Feedback Mechanisms:** Establish mechanisms to gather feedback from customers in the new locations. Use surveys, social media, or in-person interactions to understand customer preferences.
- **Customer Loyalty Programs:** Introduce loyalty programs or discounts for repeat customers to foster customer retention.

11. Operational Efficiency:

- **Standardized Processes:** Maintain standardized operating processes across locations to ensure consistency in food quality and service.
- **Supply Chain Coordination:** Coordinate with suppliers to ensure a smooth and reliable supply chain, minimizing disruptions in the new locations.

12. Event Planning:

- **Event Selection Criteria:** Evaluate events based on their alignment with your target audience, scale, and potential return on investment.
- **Event Logistics:** Plan logistics for events, considering factors such as space requirements, electricity access, and foot traffic.

13. Health and Safety Protocols:

- **COVID-19 Considerations:** Implement health and safety protocols, especially in light of the ongoing COVID-19 pandemic. Consider contactless payment options and safe food handling practices.
- **Emergency Preparedness:** Have contingency plans in place for emergencies, such as extreme weather conditions or unexpected closures.

14. Community Involvement:

- **Community Events:** Participate in local community events to integrate your food truck into the neighborhood and build a positive reputation.
- **Sponsorships:** Explore sponsorship opportunities for local sports teams, festivals, or charitable events to enhance community engagement.

15. Data Analytics and Performance Monitoring:

- **Performance Metrics:** Establish key performance indicators (KPIs) to measure the success of the expansion, such as sales growth, customer satisfaction, and return on investment.
- **Data Analytics Tools:** Use data analytics tools to track sales trends, customer preferences, and operational efficiency in each location.

16. Flexibility and Adaptability:

- **Adapt to Feedback:** Be open to feedback from customers and staff, and be willing to make adjustments to better align with local preferences.

- **Real-Time Decision Making:** Develop a flexible mindset and the ability to make real-time decisions to address challenges or capitalize on opportunities.

17. Sustainability Initiatives:

- **Environmentally Friendly Practices:** Implement sustainability initiatives, such as eco-friendly packaging or waste reduction measures, to align with local and global trends.
- **Community Impact:** Communicate your commitment to sustainability, contributing to positive community relations.

18. Evaluate Return on Investment (ROI):

- **ROI Analysis:** Regularly assess the return on investment for each new location or event. Evaluate the effectiveness of marketing strategies, menu changes, and overall operational performance.

19. Customer Education:

- **Educate Customers:** If your food offerings are unique or unfamiliar to the local market, provide information to educate customers about your cuisine and specialties.

- **Tasting Events:** Consider hosting tasting events or samplings to introduce your food to the new audience.

20. Social Media Presence:

- **Localized Social Media Campaigns:** Leverage social media platforms with localized campaigns to create buzz and engage with the community.
- **User-Generated Content:** Encourage customers to share their experiences on social media, creating user-generated content that promotes your brand.

21. Quality Control:

- **Consistent Quality:** Ensure that all locations provide food and service that meets a high standard. Put quality control procedures in place to guarantee consistency.
- **Frequent Audits:** To ensure adherence to health and safety regulations, conduct routine audits or inspections.

22. Test and Learn Approach:

- **Pilot Programs:** Consider piloting your food truck in a new location or at specific events before committing to a long-term presence.
- **Iterative Improvement:** Use a test-and-learn approach, continuously gathering

insights and making iterative improvements based on performance data.

23. Local Trends and Cultural Sensitivity:

- **Stay Informed:** Stay informed about local trends, cultural nuances, and events to tailor your offerings and marketing strategies accordingly.
- **Cultural Sensitivity:** Be culturally sensitive and respectful to the diverse preferences of the local population.

24. Networking and Relationship Building:

- **Local Business Associations:** Join local business associations or networks to connect with other businesses and gain insights into the community.
- **Relationships with Authorities:** Establish positive relationships with local authorities, event organizers, and community leaders to facilitate smooth operations.

25. Brand Visibility:

- **Strategic Locations:** Choose strategic locations that maximize brand visibility. Consider high-traffic areas, popular landmarks, or locations with limited food options.

- **Branded Merchandise:** Introduce branded merchandise to enhance brand visibility and create additional revenue streams.

26. Scaling Operations Gradually:

- **Incremental Growth:** Consider scaling operations gradually, especially when entering new markets. Assess performance and demand before committing to full-scale expansion.
- **Pilot Programs:** Launch pilot programs to test the waters and gather insights that inform future expansion decisions.

27. Cross-Promotion with Existing Locations:

- **Leverage Existing Customer Base:** Cross-promote the new locations or events to your existing customer base through social media, email newsletters, or loyalty programs.
- **Customer Incentives:** Offer special promotions or incentives for customers to visit the new locations, creating a seamless transition.

28. Adaptability to Seasonal Changes:

- **Seasonal Adjustments:** Be prepared to adapt your offerings and operating hours to seasonal changes. Consider seasonal specialties or themed events to attract customers.

- **Weather Considerations:** Factor in weather conditions when planning events, ensuring that your food truck can operate effectively in various conditions.

29. Strategic Alliances:

- **Alliances with Local Businesses:** Form alliances with local businesses that complement your food truck offerings. For example, collaborate with a coffee shop for morning events or a dessert shop for evening events.
- **Mutually Beneficial Partnerships:** Seek partnerships that are mutually beneficial, creating value for both your food truck and the partnering business.

30. Post-Expansion Evaluation:

- **Post-Expansion Review:** After the initial period of expansion, conduct a comprehensive review of the performance of each new location or event.
- **Lessons Learned:** Identify lessons learned, successes, and areas for improvement. Apply these insights to refine your expansion strategy for future initiatives.

Expanding your food truck to new locations and events requires a blend of strategic planning, adaptability, and a deep understanding of local markets. By carefully considering the unique characteristics of each location, staying attuned to customer preferences, and continuously evaluating and adapting your approach, you can successfully grow your food truck business and build a strong presence in diverse markets.

8.2: Collaborations and partnerships

Collaborations and partnerships can be powerful strategies for enhancing the reach, brand visibility, and overall success of your food truck business. By joining forces with other businesses, organizations, or individuals, you can tap into new customer bases, leverage shared resources, and create unique offerings. Here's a detailed guide on how to develop and navigate collaborations and partnerships for your food truck:

1. Identify Potential Partners:

- **Complementary Businesses:** Seek for companies or groups that will enhance your food truck offerings. For instance, if your area of expertise is savoury foods, think about collaborating with a dessert provider.

- **Local Businesses:** Explore collaborations with other local businesses, such as coffee shops, breweries, or event venues.

2. Understand Mutual Benefits:

- **Shared Audience:** Identify how a potential collaboration can expose your food truck to a new and relevant audience.
- **Mutual Value:** Ensure that both parties derive value from the collaboration, whether it's through increased sales, brand exposure, or shared resources.

3. Define Clear Objectives:

- **Specific Goals:** Clearly define the objectives and goals of the collaboration. Whether it's expanding your customer base, launching a joint promotion, or enhancing the overall customer experience, having clear goals is essential.

4. Build Strong Relationships:

- **Open Communication:** Establish open lines of communication with potential partners. Transparent and honest communication is key to building strong and lasting relationships.

- **Networking:** To find possible partners and establish contacts, go to industry conferences, networking events, or local business activities.

5. Legal Agreements:

- **Partnership Agreement:** Draft a formal partnership agreement that outlines the terms and expectations of the collaboration. This may include revenue sharing, responsibilities, and the duration of the partnership.
- **Legal Consultation:** Seek legal advice to ensure that all aspects of the collaboration are legally sound and protect the interests of both parties.

6. Types of Collaborations:

- **Cross-Promotions:** Partner with another business to cross-promote each other's products or services. For instance, offer discounts to each other's customers.
- **Co-Branding:** Explore co-branding opportunities where both businesses contribute to a joint product or experience, creating a unique offering.

7. Community Collaborations:

- **Local Events and Organizations:** Collaborate with local events, festivals, or community organizations. Participating in or sponsoring local events can increase your food truck's visibility.
- **Charitable Collaborations:** Partner with charitable organizations for events or campaigns. This not only supports a good cause but also enhances your brand's reputation.

8. Create Unique Experiences:

- **Themed Events:** Collaborate on themed events or promotions to create a memorable experience for customers.
- **Exclusive Menus:** Develop exclusive menu items or collaborations that are only available during the partnership period.

9. Strategic Alliances:

- **Leverage Resources:** Form strategic alliances where businesses with complementary resources, such as a shared kitchen space or supplier connections, collaborate to maximize efficiency.
- **Cost-Sharing:** Explore cost-sharing arrangements to reduce expenses, especially for joint marketing efforts or events.

10. Social Media Collaboration:

- **Joint Social Media Campaigns:** Plan joint social media campaigns to cross-promote each other's businesses. This can include giveaways, featured posts, or collaborative content.
- **Tagging and Mentioning:** Encourage customers to tag both businesses when sharing their collaboration experiences on social media.

11. Event Collaborations:

- **Food and Beverage Pairings:** Collaborate with a beverage provider for unique food and beverage pairings at events or in your regular service.
- **Pop-Up Collaborations:** Organize pop-up collaborations with other vendors or businesses to create buzz and attract a diverse audience.

12. Promotional Activities:

- **Joint Discounts:** Offer joint discounts or promotions for customers who make purchases from both collaborating businesses.
- **Limited-Time Offers:** Introduce limited-time offers that highlight the collaboration

and create a sense of urgency for customers to try something new.

13. Feedback and Evaluation:

- **Post-Collaboration Evaluation:** After a collaboration, gather feedback from both parties to evaluate its success. Identify what worked well and areas for improvement.
- **Customer Feedback:** Seek customer feedback to understand their response to the collaboration and whether it positively impacted their experience.

14. Online Platforms and Apps:

- **Food Delivery Apps:** Partner with food delivery apps for promotions or featured listings that can increase your food truck's visibility.
- **Collaborative Online Campaigns:** Engage in joint online campaigns with other businesses, leveraging their online presence for mutual promotion.

15. Employee Engagement:

- **Staff Training:** If collaboration involves joint events or promotions, ensure that staff from both businesses are trained to provide a seamless and positive customer experience.

- **Team Building:** Collaborate on team-building activities or events to strengthen the bond between your staff and your collaborating partner's team.

16. Collective Marketing Efforts:

- **Shared Marketing Materials:** Create shared marketing materials, such as flyers or digital assets, to promote the collaboration consistently.
- **Email Marketing Campaigns:** Include collaborative promotions in email marketing campaigns to reach a broader audience.

17. Local Influencers and Bloggers:

- **Engage Local Influencers:** Collaborate with local influencers or bloggers to amplify the reach of your joint efforts.
- **User-Generated Content:** Encourage customers to share their experiences on social media, creating user-generated content that showcases the collaboration.

18. Exclusivity Agreements:

- **Exclusive Collaborations:** Consider exclusivity agreements for certain collaborations, ensuring that both parties benefit from a unique and differentiated offering.

- **Duration and Terms:** Clearly define the duration and terms of exclusivity to prevent conflicts or misunderstandings.

19. Evaluating Brand Alignment:

- **Brand Values:** Ensure that collaborating businesses share similar values and standards to maintain brand consistency.
- **Target Audience Alignment:** Verify that both businesses' target audiences align to maximize the impact of the collaboration.

20. Post-Collaboration Marketing:

- **Content Creation:** Use content created during the collaboration, such as videos, photos, or testimonials, in post-collaboration marketing efforts.
- **Highlight Success Stories:** Share success stories and customer feedback from the collaboration through various marketing channels.

21. Networking Events:

- **Industry Networking:** Attend industry-specific networking events or conferences to identify potential collaboration opportunities within your sector.

- **Local Business Associations:** Join local business associations or chambers of commerce to connect with other businesses in your area.

22. Flexibility and Adaptability:

- **Adapt to Changes:** Be flexible and adaptable in the collaboration process. Markets, trends, and business conditions may change, requiring adjustments to collaboration strategies.
- **Iterative Improvement:** Use feedback and insights from previous collaborations to continuously improve future initiatives.

23. Cross-Promotion through Packaging:

- **Co-Branded Packaging:** Explore co-branded packaging that promotes both collaborating businesses and offers a cohesive and visually appealing product.
- **Incorporate Branding Elements:** Incorporate branding elements from both businesses on packaging materials for a unified look.

24. Collaboration Announcements:

- **Engaging Launch:** Create engaging launch announcements for collaborations to generate excitement and anticipation among your customer base.
- **Teasers and Sneak Peeks:** Utilize teasers or sneak peeks on social media to build anticipation before officially launching the collaboration.

25. Monitoring and Analytics:

- **Key Performance Indicators (KPIs):** Establish KPIs to monitor the success of collaborations, such as sales growth, customer engagement, or social media reach.
- **Data Analytics:** Use data analytics tools to track the performance of collaborative efforts and identify areas for improvement.

26. Educational Collaborations:

- **Workshops or Classes:** Collaborate on educational events, such as cooking workshops or classes, that offer value to customers beyond the usual product offerings.
- **Skill Exchange:** Exchange skills or expertise with collaborating partners, fostering a learning environment for both parties.

27. Crisis Communication Plans:

- **Prepare for Contingencies:** Develop crisis communication plans in case of unforeseen challenges or negative outcomes from collaborations.
- **Quick Response:** Be prepared to respond quickly to any issues, demonstrating transparency and a commitment to addressing concerns.

28. International Collaborations:

- **Cultural Sensitivity:** If collaborating with businesses from different cultures or countries, be culturally sensitive and aware of any cultural nuances that may impact the collaboration.
- **Legal Considerations:** Understand international legal considerations, including regulations and trade agreements that may affect collaborations.

29. Performance Reviews:

- **Regular Reviews:** Conduct regular performance reviews of collaborative efforts to assess their impact on both businesses.
- **Continuous Improvement:** Use performance feedback to identify areas for improvement and enhance the effectiveness of future collaborations.

30. Maintain Long-Term Relationships:

- **Nurture Relationships:** For long-term success, actively cultivate your relationships with partners. Celebrate victories as a group and work together to overcome obstacles.
- **Ongoing Communication:** Maintain ongoing communication to stay informed about each other's business activities and identify new opportunities for collaboration.

Collaborations and partnerships can be transformative for your food truck business, providing opportunities for growth, innovation, and enhanced customer experiences. By approaching collaborations strategically, fostering strong relationships, and adapting to changing market dynamics, you can leverage these partnerships to create a lasting impact on your business's success.

8.3: Scaling up operations and considerations for a brick-and-mortar establishment

Scaling up operations from a food truck to a brick-and-mortar establishment is a significant step that requires careful planning, strategic decision-making, and operational adjustments. The transition involves moving from a mobile and compact setup to a more permanent and larger space. Here's a detailed guide on how to scale up operations for a brick-and-mortar establishment:

1. Market Research and Location Selection:

- **Demographics Analysis:** Conduct thorough market research to understand the demographics, preferences, and buying behavior of the target customer base in the selected area.
- **Location Considerations:** Choose a location with high foot traffic, proximity to your target audience, and minimal competition. Assess factors such as parking availability and visibility.

2. Financial Planning and Funding:

- **Budgeting:** Develop a detailed budget that includes costs for leasing or purchasing the space, interior renovations, equipment, licenses, permits, marketing, and initial operating expenses.
- **Funding Sources:** Explore funding options, including loans, investors, crowdfunding, or personal savings. Consider the financial impact during the transition period.

3. Legal and Regulatory Compliance:

- **Permits and Licenses:** Ensure compliance with all necessary permits and licenses for a brick-and-mortar establishment. This may include health permits, building permits, and occupancy licenses.
- **Zoning Regulations:** Verify that the chosen location complies with zoning regulations for a restaurant or food service establishment.

4. Menu Development and Adaptation:

- **Expanded Menu Options:** Consider expanding your menu to provide a wider variety of options to attract a broader customer base.
- **Pricing Strategy:** Evaluate and adjust your pricing strategy to reflect the new operational costs associated with a brick-and-mortar establishment.

5. Interior Design and Layout:

- **Functional Layout:** Plan an efficient and functional layout that optimizes space for both kitchen and customer seating areas.
- **Aesthetics and Branding:** Design the interior to reflect your brand identity. Consider hiring professionals for interior design to create an inviting and cohesive atmosphere.

6. Equipment and Technology:

- **Upgraded Kitchen Equipment:** Invest in high-quality and larger kitchen equipment suitable for increased production capacity.
- **Point-of-Sale (POS) System:** Implement a robust POS system that can handle the complexities of a brick-and-mortar setting, including order processing, inventory management, and sales tracking.

7. Staffing and Training:

- **Hiring Staff:** Recruit additional staff to handle the expanded operations. This may include kitchen staff, servers, and front-of-house personnel.
- **Training Programs:** Develop comprehensive training programs to ensure that staff members are well-versed in the new operational procedures and customer service expectations.

8. Supply Chain Management:

- **Vendor Relationships:** Review and renegotiate contracts with suppliers to accommodate increased demand and potentially negotiate better pricing.

- **Inventory Management:** Implement effective inventory management systems to prevent stockouts and minimize waste.

9. Marketing and Branding:

- **Local Marketing Campaigns:** Launch local marketing campaigns to announce the opening of your brick-and-mortar establishment. Utilize both online and traditional marketing channels.
- **Consistent Branding:** Ensure that your branding remains consistent across all platforms, including signage, menus, and promotional materials.

10. Customer Experience Enhancement:

- **Customer Service Standards:** Establish and communicate high standards for customer service. Train staff to provide a positive and consistent customer experience.
- **Feedback Mechanisms:** Implement systems for gathering customer feedback and use this information to make continuous improvements.

11. Operational Processes and Systems:

- **Standard Operating Procedures (SOPs):** Develop SOPs for all aspects of operations, including kitchen processes, customer service, and cleanliness standards.

- **Efficiency Improvements:** Identify opportunities for operational efficiency and implement streamlined processes to handle increased volume.

12. Technology Integration:

- **Online Ordering Systems:** Implement online ordering systems to cater to customer preferences for digital ordering.
- **Reservation Systems:** If applicable, consider implementing reservation systems for customer convenience and efficient seating management.

13. Quality Control Measures:

- **Consistent Quality Standards:** Maintain consistent quality standards for your food. Implement quality control measures to ensure that the taste and presentation meet customer expectations.
- **Regular Audits:** Conduct regular audits to assess and maintain food safety standards.

14. Community Engagement:

- **Local Partnerships:** Foster partnerships with local businesses, community organizations, or schools to enhance community engagement.

- **Opening Events:** Organize opening events or collaborations with local influencers to create buzz and attract initial customers.

15. Technology for Customer Engagement:

- **Loyalty Programs:** To promote repeat business, put in place loyalty programmes. Use technology to create applications or digital loyalty cards.
- **Customer Relationship Management (CRM):** Track customer preferences with CRM systems to offer tailored advertisements and promotions.

16. Adaptability to Customer Feedback:

- **Feedback Loops:** Establish feedback loops to gather input from customers on the menu, service, and overall experience.
- **Adaptation to Preferences:** Be willing to adapt your offerings based on customer feedback and changing preferences.

17. Strategic Pricing Adjustments:

- **Pricing Strategies:** Evaluate and adjust pricing strategies based on the cost structure of a brick-and-mortar establishment. Consider factors such as rent, utilities, and increased staffing costs.

18. Diversification of Revenue Streams:

- **Catering Services:** Explore catering opportunities to diversify revenue streams. Leverage existing customer relationships to offer catering services for events and parties.
- **Merchandising:** Introduce merchandise such as branded merchandise, sauces, or packaged products to generate additional revenue.

19. Data Analytics and Performance Monitoring:

- **Key Performance Indicators (KPIs):** Establish KPIs to measure the performance of the brick-and-mortar establishment. This may include sales growth, customer retention, and average transaction value.
- **Data Analytics Tools:** Use data analytics tools to gain insights into customer behavior, popular menu items, and operational efficiency.

20. Employee Recognition and Retention Programs:

- **Recognition Programs:** To recognise and honour exceptional work, put in place staff recognition programmes.

- **Retention Strategies:** Develop strategies to retain skilled and dedicated staff, such as providing opportunities for career growth and creating a positive work environment.

21. Compliance with Health and Safety Standards:

- **Health and Safety Protocols:** Establish and communicate health and safety protocols to comply with regulations and reassure customers.
- **Employee Training:** Train staff on hygiene practices and safety measures to maintain a clean and safe environment.

22. Strategic Marketing for New Location:

- **Local SEO Optimization:** Optimize online presence for local SEO to ensure your establishment appears in local search results.
- **Grand Opening Events:** Plan grand opening events to attract attention and generate excitement among the local community.

23. Cross-Promotions and Collaborations:

- **Local Business Collaborations:** Collaborate with other local businesses for cross-promotions and joint marketing efforts.

- **Event Sponsorships:** Sponsor local events to enhance brand visibility and community engagement.

24. Employee Cross-Training:

- **Cross-Training Programs:** Implement cross-training programs to ensure that employees are versatile and capable of handling various roles within the establishment.
- **Efficiency and Flexibility:** Cross-training enhances operational efficiency and provides flexibility during busy periods.

25. Sustainability Initiatives:

- **Environmental Practices:** Integrate sustainability initiatives into your operations, such as eco-friendly packaging or waste reduction measures.
- **Community Impact:** Communicate your commitment to sustainability, aligning with contemporary consumer preferences.

26. Adaptation to Seasonal Changes:

- **Seasonal Menu Offerings:** Adjust your menu seasonally to cater to changing tastes and preferences.

- **Seasonal Promotions:** Create promotions or events around seasonal themes to attract customers during specific times of the year.

27. Monitoring and Adapting to Trends:

- **Industry Trends:** Stay informed about industry trends and incorporate popular trends into your menu or marketing strategies.
- **Customer Preferences:** Regularly assess customer preferences and adapt your offerings to meet changing demands.

28. Customer Education Programs:

- **Tasting Events:** Host tasting events or workshops to educate customers about your cuisine, ingredients, and unique offerings.
- **Menu Explanations:** Provide clear explanations of menu items to enhance the dining experience for customers who may be trying your cuisine for the first time.

29. Participation in Food Festivals and Events:

- **Showcasing at Events:** Participate in local food festivals or events to showcase your brick-and-mortar establishment and attract a wider audience.

- **Collaborative Events:** Collaborate with other vendors or businesses for joint participation in events.

30. Continuous Improvement Culture:

- **Feedback Culture:** Foster a culture of continuous improvement based on customer feedback, employee insights, and operational assessments.
- **Regular Evaluation:** Regularly evaluate the performance of the brick-and-mortar establishment and make strategic adjustments as needed.

Growing operations to a physical location necessitates a methodical approach that takes into account a number of factors, including customer experience, financial planning, market dynamics, and operational efficiency. You may effectively create a significant presence in the brick-and-mortar restaurant market by carefully managing this shift and remaining aware of the needs of your target audience.

www.ingramcontent.com/pod-product-compliance
Lightning Source LLC
Chambersburg PA
CBHW071042290526
45795CB00004B/1283